The Market for Remittance Services in the Czech Republic

Outcomes of a Survey among Migrants

Marco Nicolì
Carlo Corazza

THE WORLD BANK
Washington, D.C.

Copyright © 2010
The International Bank for Reconstruction and Development / The World Bank
1818 H Street NW
Washington DC 20433
Telephone: 202-473-1000
Internet: www.worldbank.org

1 2 3 4   13 12 11 10

World Bank Studies are published to communicate the results of the Bank's work to the development community with the least possible delay. The manuscript of this paper therefore has not been prepared in accordance with the procedures appropriate to formally-edited texts. Some sources cited in this paper may be informal documents that are not readily available. This volume is a product of the staff of the International Bank for Reconstruction and Development/ The World Bank. The findings, interpretations, and conclusions expressed in this volume do not necessarily reflect the views of the Executive Directors of The World Bank or the governments they represent.

The World Bank does not guarantee the accuracy of the data included in this work. The boundaries, colors, denominations, and other information shown on any map in this work do not imply any judgment on the part of The World Bank concerning the legal status of any territory or the endorsement or acceptance of such boundaries.

Rights and Permissions

ISBN: 978-0-8213-8585-2
eISBN: 978-0-8213-8586-9
DOI: 10.1596/978-0-8213-8585-2

Library of Congress Cataloging-in-Publication Data
The market for remittance services in the Czech Republic : outcomes of a survey among migrants.
    p. cm.
Includes indexes.
ISBN 978-0-8213-8585-2
1. Emigrant remittances—Czech Republic. 2. Emigration and immigration—Economic aspects—Czech Republic. I. World Bank.
HG3947.3.M37 2010
332'.04246094371—dc22
                                                                    2010034794

Contents

List of Tables

List of Figures

List of Boxes

Abstract

This survey was conducted by the World Bank Payment Systems Development Group, at the request of the Ministry of Finance of the Czech Republic, as a follow up to the World Bank-led mission that visited the country in 2008 to assess the market for remittances. This survey aims at analyzing the main characteristics of the market for remittances in the Czech Republic and should serve as a guide for both public authorities and the private sector in identifying possible actions to improve the efficiency of the market.

A total of 880 migrants from eight different nationalities were interviewed during the summer of 2009 in Prague. The nationalities selected represent the largest and most important migrant communities in the country: China, Moldova, Mongolia, Poland, the Russian Federation, the Slovak Republic, Ukraine, and Vietnam.

The following main findings can be extracted from the analysis of the survey's outcomes:

- A low level of transparency and consumer protection can be observed in the market for remittances in the Czech Republic. Senders are often not provided with all the relevant information by the Remittance Service Provider (RSP) at the moment of the transaction.
- The lack of transparency is confirmed by the analysis of the cost as perceived by the interviewees, who do not generally consider the margin applied by the RSP as a price component. As a result, remittance senders are in general not aware of the actual cost that they are paying for the service.
- The market is dominated by Money Transfer Operators (MTOs) and, in particular, some MTOs hold the great majority of the market shares.
- Banks and the post office represent a largely unused resource for remitting money. In particular, migrants seem to be interested in banks' services, but they are discouraged from using them due to high costs, slowness of transfers, and lack of specific services offered by banks.
- A considerable portion of remittance flows through informal[1] channels, such as friends or relatives travelling to the home countries, regular mail, or bus drivers. Even though relatively slower, less transparent, and less safe, these services are used by a large portion of migrants because of the low costs and easy access.

Note

[1] The distinction between the formal and informal sector is controversial. In this report, this distinction is used with the sole purpose of isolating data that concern RSPs by other methods of sending money. For additional information, see note 9, page 23.

Acknowledgments

This study *"The market for remittance services in the Czech Republic: Outcomes of a Survey among Migrants"* is the result of the efforts of the Payment Systems Development Group (PSDG) of the World Bank. The data and conclusions presented in this study, including the detailed questionnaire that was used to survey migrant communities in the Czech Republic, were produced by a team under the leadership of Carlo Corazza (Financial Sector Specialist, PSDG). Other team members included Massimo Cirasino (Head, PSDG), who supervised and provided guidance on various steps of this project, and Marco Nicolì (Payment System and Remittances Analyst, PSDG), who coordinated the field work, provided key support in the processing and analysis of qualitative and quantitative data, and was instrumental in the various follow-up efforts to organize the information. The PSDG worked in coordination with the Inter-American Dialogue (IAD) to develop the adequate methodology for the interviews, under the guidance and expertise of Dr. Manuel Orozco (Senior Associate, IAD) and Nancy Castillo (Program Assistant, IAD).

A team of nine interviewers in the Czech Republic undertook the essential work of the data gathering and allowed the coordination with the migrant communities: Ms. Ting Ting Chen, Mr. Nicolae Cherdivara, Ms. Hoa Dang, Mr. Tuvshinbat Dorj, Ms. Olga Evseeva, Ms. Jana Glogarova, Ms. Hanna Ludkiewcz, Mr. Petr Mederly, and Ms. Dagmar Silná.

The Ministry of Finance of the Czech Republic provided funds, encouragement and essential logistic support before, during and after the implementation phase. Ms. Eva Anderova (Director, EU and International Relations Department) strongly believed in the project and its importance for the overall improvement of the market for remittance in the Czech Republic. Ms. Ivana Vlkova (Head of the Unit—EU and International Relations Department) and her team supplied constant assistance and coordination with local authorities, foreign embassies and migrant communities.

Finally, the PSDG wishes to thank each and every migrant who participated in this effort.

Abbreviations

ACH	Automatic Clearing House
CIS	Commonwealth of Independent States
CPSS	Committee on Payment and Settlement Systems of the Bank for International Settlements (BIS)
EU	European Union
GPs	CPSS-World Bank, General Principles for International Remittance Services
IAD	Inter-American Dialogue
IOM	International Organization for Migration
MTO	Money Transfer Operator
PSDG	World Bank Payments System Development Group
RSP	Remittance Service Provider

CHAPTER 1

Introduction

In May 2008, in response to a request from the Ministry of Finance of the Czech Republic, a World Bank–led mission visited the Czech Republic to provide local authorities with a review of the market for remittances on the basis of the Committee on Payment and Settlement Systems of the Bank for International Settlements (CPSS)–World Bank General Principles on International Remittances Services (GPs) and identify possible actions to implement their application in the country. The international team delivered to the authorities a final analytical report, based on international standards and best practices. The report included some observations aimed at discussing the improvement and future development of the market for the provision of remittance services in the Czech Republic. In particular some key actions were identified that, according to World Bank's experience in other countries, could lead to a reduction in the cost of transferring money from and to the Czech Republic, and in general to safer and more efficient remittance services in the country by promoting a market that is contestable, competitive, transparent, accessible, and sound.

The Ministry of Finance, following up on the recommendations of the report, requested the Payment Systems Development Group of the World Bank (PSDG) to organize and oversee a survey on the market for remittances.

In April 2009 the PSDG started the relevant activities to undertake the task and, in cooperation with the Ministry of Finance, coordinated the implementation phase with the embassies and consulates of the most relevant migrant communities in the Czech Republic. Between July and September 2009, the PSDG deployed a team on the ground led by Mr. Marco Nicolì, analyst at the PSDG, and formed of interviewers from the eight nationalities selected for the survey.

The survey aims at analyzing the main characteristics of the market for remittances in the country through a detailed questionnaire produced by PSDG, in cooperation with the Inter-American Dialogue (IAD), a consulting firm contracted for this specific purpose. The answers to the questionnaires were statistically analyzed by the IAD and the collected data are being investigated by the PSDG.

This report analyzes the outcomes of the survey and provides a review of the market for remittance services in Czech Republic.

CHAPTER 2

Overview

Recently, the Czech Republic has moved from its history as a traditional source of immigrants, to become an attractive location for immigration from other countries. In 2009 over 430,000 foreigners were residing officially in the country according to the Ministry of the Interior, representing more than four percent of the total population. Approximately one-third of these immigrants are citizens of the European Union. Ukrainians represent about 30 percent of legal residents in the Czech Republic. Slovaks, whose links with the Czech Republic have been maintained after the division of former Czechoslovakia, account for over 17 percent. Vietnamese are the third migrant community in the Czech Republic, with 14 percent of legal residents. Other nationalities are Russians (6 percent), Polish (5 percent), Moldovans (2 percent), and Mongolians (2 percent).

Illegal immigration figures are not easily quantifiable and there are conflicting opinions on the exact number of illegal foreigners in the country. Official statistics indicate that 53,000 people illegally resided in the country in 2006.[1] However, anecdotal evidence suggests that there could be approximately 200,000 foreigners residing illegally in the country.[2]

Immigrants typically migrate to the Czech Republic for economic reasons. In the Czech Republic, 86 percent of immigrants are within the economically active age (15–59), and their age structure clearly differs from that typical of the host population. Slovaks can probably be considered an exception, since the age structure for them is more similar to the host population.

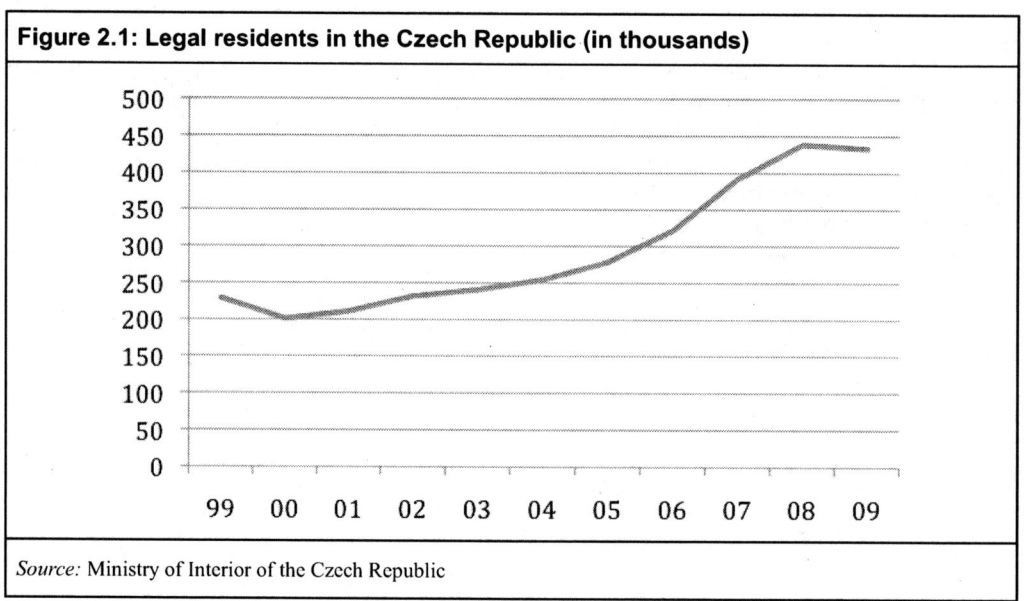

Figure 2.1: Legal residents in the Czech Republic (in thousands)

Source: Ministry of Interior of the Czech Republic

Both migration and remittances are increasingly relevant, in economic terms, for the Czech Republic. The World Bank estimates that inward remittance flows in 2008 amounted to USD 1.4 billion (0.5 percent of GDP), while outward remittance flows were equivalent to USD 3.8 billion (1.4 percent of GDP). Remittance inflows originate mainly from EU countries (85 percent) while outflows are directed toward Slovak Republic (37 percent), Ukraine (28 percent) and Vietnam (11 percent). The remaining 24 percent of the money is sent to Poland, other Commonwealth of Independent States (CIS) countries, China, and Mongolia.

At present, the main remittance service providers (RSPs) paying remittances in the Czech Republic include commercial banks, money transfer operators (MTOs), foreign exchange bureaus, cooperatives, credit unions, couriers companies, and a wide variety of commercial entities acting as correspondent agents for larger RSPs. Western Union and other smaller MTOs play a major role in the market for remittance services.

The majority of remittances seems to be disbursed through regulated service providers, especially when the sender is a legal migrant. However, a good portion of the remittance flow leaves the Czech Republic through non-institutional market players, as described below in the analysis of the outcomes of the survey. In particular, it can be assumed that most irregular residents send money back home through the so-called *clients*[3] and other non-institutional market players. There are no exact estimates of such flows, as very little information is available either from official channels or from the different migrants' communities; however, a good picture is provided by the data collected in this survey.

Banks seem to have scarce comprehension of the real scale of the remittances market and, hence, limited appetite to grab potential business opportunities. They have not adapted their internal procedures to offer personalized services to the migrant community, nor have they created new external channels or products to attract these customers. Marketing strategies are not specifically targeted towards those who remit money, as they are not seen as profitable customers. In some cases banks are excluded from the market, as some enterprises—mainly from Slovak Republic and Poland—pay their foreign employees directly in the country of origin through satellite companies, providing workers with

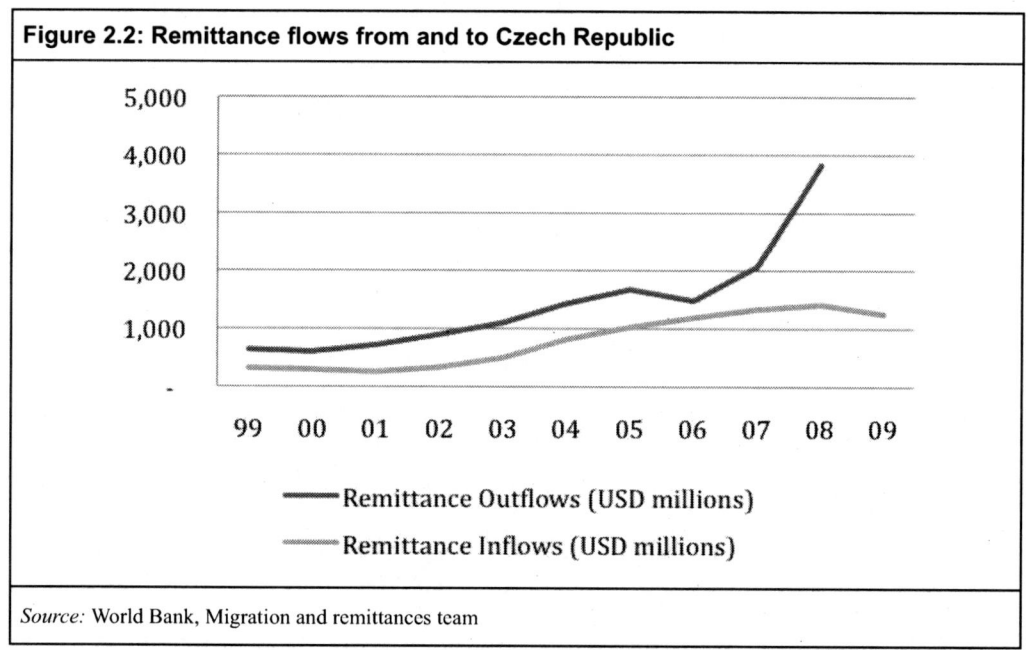

Figure 2.2: Remittance flows from and to Czech Republic

Source: World Bank, Migration and remittances team

housing, meals and general sustainment and giving them in Czech crowns only the amount necessary for small daily expenses.

Worldwide, delivery of funds to the beneficiaries generally occurs in cash. A similar assumption could be made for those countries that receive remittances from the Czech Republic. The share of remittances sent from the Czech Republic that are paid through or deposited into deposit accounts appears relatively small. Payment cards are seldom used in connection to remittances, and banks do not offer specific services or have agreements with counterparts in foreign countries to allow the reduction of the costs of direct deposit wire transfers through interconnected Automatic Clearing Houses (ACH).

The current foreign exchange law (Act no. 219/1995 Coll.) and its amendments regulate the licensing regime and monitoring and data gathering on the remittances market. The Ministry of Finance and the Czech National Bank play different roles with respect to the above-mentioned aspects of the regulation from both points of view. The market is organized in a way that remittance operations fall under some type of control by one or more authorities. In addition, RSPs are considered reporting entities according to the new Anti-Money Laundering Law, and they have to report to the Financial Analytical Unit of the Ministry of Finance all suspect transactions.

Notes

[1] Source: Directorate of Alien and Border Police, Ministry of the Interior of the Czech Republic.

[2] The International Organization for Migration (IOM) estimates that between 295,000 and 335,000 foreigners resided illegally in the country in 2000. Source: "Migration Trends in selected EU Applicant Countries,"
Vol. II: The Czech Republic; The International Organization for Migration, 2004.

[3] The term "*client*" is used informally to indicate those individuals, in particular from CIS countries, legally residing in the Czech Republic, who have built up an articulated network in the migrant community of origin and provide their fellow citizens with multiple services under the payment of fees. These services range from the research of a job, to the legal help to reside in the country, to the assistance in finding a home. *Clients* operate without any formal authorization from the Czech authorities, although sometimes might be licensed by the authorities of the country of origin. In many cases such activity can be associated with criminal conducts such as smuggling, human trafficking, prostitution and contraband. For further information, see Jan Cerník, "Of Clients and Chereps The Organizational Structures of Ukrainian Labor Migration."

CHAPTER 3

Rationale and Objectives of the Survey

The objective of the survey is to provide an analysis of the main features of the market for remittances in the Czech Republic, based on the GPs. The outcomes of the survey should serve as a guide for both public authorities and the private sector in carrying out further investigations and identifying possible actions to improve the efficiency of the market for remittances in the country.

The survey serves as a reference for the Czech authorities in the identification of those constraints, problems, and inefficiencies that might be hampering the reliable, fair, and low-priced flow of remittances from and to the country. Additionally, the survey helps to identify the potentialities and resources for the improvement of competition, increase the level of transparency, and guarantee a better protection of migrants' rights. Public authorities can use the findings in the survey as a guide for their action in reforming the retail payments system infrastructure of the country and in fostering the use of alternative and more efficient ways to send and receive money. Authorities might also decide to adopt more incisive policies in the area of financial literacy and dissemination of the information, tailoring their intervention in a more precise and defined way.

The survey is also aimed at representing a useful instrument for the private sector to better understand the business opportunities available in the market and shed the light on those marketing activities that, according to several other international experiences, can lead the private sector to play an increasing role in the collection and disbursement of remittances. By gathering relevant information on the opinions, reluctances, and problems of the migrants, the survey highlights the possible immediate interventions that banks, MTOs, the postal service, and the other financial institutions providing remittances services can adopt to increase the number of their customers and to offer them other financial products that could be linked to remittances. This would have an immediate impact not only on the total flows channeled through a reliable and convenient system, but also on the number of migrants having access to bank accounts, loans, insurances, and other financial services.

Finally, the survey represents the ideal starting point for the implementation of more concrete and practical tools: among others, the creation of a national database on the cost of sending remittances from the Czech Republic. The detailed description of the features of the market offer to the researchers and to the authorities the advantage of having a solid base on which to start this specific investigation. It allows a shorter process of adjustment to the reality of the market.

CHAPTER 4

Methodology

The survey was collected during the months of July and August 2009. The PSDG, in cooperation with the IAD, trained the interviewers, coordinated the work in the field and monitored the submission and administration of the questionnaires. The team collected a total of 880 interviews, 110 per each of the eight selected nationalities. All the interviews were conducted person to person and the interviewees were selected randomly, according to statistically validated sampling methods.

Demographic Sample

The survey analyzes the market for remittances for the eight largest and most important migrant communities in the Czech Republic. The numeric and social relevance of the migrant communities was established according to official data, data collected by the World Bank on the ground, and in consultation with the relevant authorities of the Czech government (in particular, Ministry of Finance, Ministry of Interior, Czech Statistical Office, Czech National Bank).

The nationalities selected for the survey are China, Moldova, Mongolia, Poland, Russia, Slovak Republic, Ukraine, and Vietnam. Table 4.1 shows the number of legal migrants for these nationalities.

Table 4.1: Number of migrants holding a residence permit per nationalities

Nationality	Number of Migrants
Ukraine	131,965
Slovak Republic *	76,034
Vietnam	60,258
Russia	27,176
Poland *	21,710
Moldova	10,644
Mongolia	8,569
China	5,239

Source: Ministry of Interior of the Czech Republic

* Figures above only include foreign nationals who were issued a permanent or a long-term residence permit. EU citizens have the right to reside in the Czech Republic with no permit. The numbers above only include EU citizens who applied for or were issued a special resident permit by Czech authorities. Thus, the number of EU citizens, residing in the Czech Republic is considerably higher than the one shown in the table. Also, due to the common history of Slovak Republic and Czech Republic, many Slovaks hold Czech citizenship and may not be represented in the figure above. According to Slovak migrant associations in Prague, there may be over 350,000 Slovaks residing in the Czech Republic, most of them being permanent and legal residents.

Table 4.2: Age, time in Czech Republic, and income, by nationality

	China	Moldova	Mongolia	Poland	Russia	Slovak Republic	Ukraine	Vietnam	Total
Average age	34	33	32	36	37	34	37	34	35
Average years in the country	7	5	3	4	6	7	4	7	5
Average annual income (USD)	13,418	13,399	7,898	19,746	17,489	19,884	13,699	11,302	13,471

The Czech Republic offers a variety of migration patterns that allow for an analysis of the market for remittances particularly varied.

The inclusion of the Slovak community in the survey aims at understanding whether the recent historical link between the two countries has left either specific advantages or constraints in the cross border flow of money, in particular when compared to Poland, another neighboring member of the European Union.

Historically the Czech Republic has maintained important political ties with Vietnam and this has made possible the development of a long-time established Vietnamese community in the country. From the same region, Chinese and Mongolians represent smaller but fast-growing communities. The selection of these three nationalities allows for a comparison among remittance flows directed to the same area of the world, but with different originating patterns.

Similarly, the analysis of the features of the market for remittances towards former Soviet countries such as Russia, Ukraine, and Moldova, aims not only at capturing data for the largest migrant community in the country (i.e., Ukraine) but at highlighting the specificities of two fundamental communities: the Russian, wealthier and established in the country for a longer time, and the Moldovan, poorer and greatly dependent on the flows of remittances from abroad.

Surveyed migrants are on average 35 years old, and they have been living in the Czech Republic for five years. Chinese, Slovak, and Vietnamese migrants have lived the longest time in the country, for approximately seven years on average. Mongolians represent the most recently established community, with an average presence in the Czech Republic of three years.

Disparities exist in income across different country of origin. Migrants' average annual income is below USD 14,000. Citizens from the bordering countries, such as the Slovak Republic and Poland, earn the highest annual income at nearly USD 20,000. Citizens from Mongolia, China and Vietnam have the lowest annual incomes (see table 4.2).

Interviewers

In order to obtain the maximum confidence in the process from the interviewed migrants and avoid any linguistic and terminological misunderstandings, interviewers were selected according to their nationality and fluency in the same language as the migrant group they had to interview. For the Slovak Republic and Poland, two interviewers were selected for each migrant group, while in the case of Russia, questionnaires were collected by the interviewers from Ukraine and Moldova.[1]

The following criteria were used to select the interviewers:

■ Motivation, interest in migration, remittances, and finance
■ Knowledge of survey administration and previous experience in similar projects

- Ability to use MS Excel
- Ability to approach people without being biased and gain trust from strangers
- Language nativity of the migrants' group to be interviewed and fluency in English

The interviewers attended three days of training, during which the PSDG and the IAD provided them with all the relevant guidance on the remittance market and survey administration. In particular, during the first day, interviewers were introduced to the project background and provided with an overview of the main topics related to the project, in particular:

- Definition of remittance
- Cost structure for remittance services
- Role of the World Bank
- Overview of the market for remittance services in the Czech Republic

Interviewers were then provided with all the relevant information on survey administration, logistics, and methodology. The questionnaire was accurately explained in all its parts, question by question.

The second day of training was dedicated to practice: interviewers were invited to interview each other, common mistakes were identified and best practices highlighted.

On the third day, interviewers started practicing the submission of the questionnaire in the field, under the direct supervision of the trainers. In the afternoon, lessons learned were shared. Finally, interviewers were instructed how to input the answers into a MS Excel template provided by the trainers.

Sampling Method

Individuals to be interviewed were selected randomly in order to ensure that the sample would not be biased. Two filter questions were included in the questionnaire in order to detect only migrants: (a) from the selected nationalities, (b) who sent money to their home countries.

The interviewers were instructed to attempt surveying every third person passing by their designated location, counting only passersby who could be from the nationality of interest. If the selected person declined or did not pass one of the filter-questions, the interviewers would ask the next person they thought could come from the country of interest. Then, the interviewer would resume asking every third person. The number of people counted before selecting the interviewee was adjusted for low-density locations, where the interviewer could stop each second person.[2]

The interviews were carried out orally, in the native language of the interviewee while the questionnaires were filled out in English by the interviewers. The migrants were assured that the answers would remain anonymous. The interviewers were properly trained to engage in an organic conversation with the interviewee, in order to gain his or her trust and make the whole process seem quicker.

Locations

About one hundred locations were selected in the Prague metropolitan area. Locations included squares, transportation hubs, shopping centers and stores, retail and wholesale markets, restaurants and bars, workplaces, consular offices, churches, and residential areas.

Locations were identified with the help of the embassies and consulates of each surveyed nationality and in consultation with each interviewer's personal experience. The

World Bank coordinator visited the most important locations before starting the collection of the questionnaires, in order to ensure their adequacy to the purpose.

Each interviewer was provided with the complete list of locations and instructed to visit as many of them as possible, in order to ensure diversity in the sample.

Locations were classified by density (low, medium, high) and by distance from the center of Prague (within 30 minutes, within one hour, more than one hour). Only in the case of Mongolia was it necessary to visit locations more than one hour from the center of Prague, due to the low concentration of Mongolians in the city.

Notes

[1] Notwithstanding the strong presence of Slovaks in the Czech Republic, it was surprisingly challenging to find Slovak nationals qualified to work as interviewers. Thus, two Czech nationals were selected. Finding an interviewer for Russia was difficult as well. However, the interviewers from Ukraine and Moldova were both native Russian-language speakers, and this qualified them for the collection of questionnaires among Russians.
[2] This method allows building a truly random sample, not affected by the judgment of the interviewer, who may naturally try to interview passersby who look easier to approach.

CHAPTER 5

Outcomes of the Survey

This section provides an analysis of the data collected through the survey.

Sending Money from the Czech Republic

The survey shows that migrants in the Czech Republic remit an average of USD 353 per transaction, five times per year. Respondents send on average 13 percent of their annual income. The average amount remitted per year is USD 1,808.

Among the nationalities surveyed, Slovaks and Poles earn the highest annual income, followed by Russians, while Mongolians declared the lowest income. This is confirmed by anecdotal evidence, as Slovak, Poles, and Russians are notoriously the wealthiest migrant communities in the Czech Republic and Mongolians are generally manual workers in the automotive or food industries.

Chinese send the highest percentage of their income back home (30 percent), followed by Mongolians (22 percent). However, it was particularly challenging to obtain information on the annual income of Chinese migrants, as many of them refused to respond to this question;[1] thus, the very high percentage of annual income remitted might be biased. Russians and Ukrainians are the ones remitting the lowest percentage of their income (respectively, 7 and 9 percent).

Transfers do not seem to vary by gender, as both men and women remit about the same portion of their income, even though the net amount remitted by men is higher, as their average annual income is generally higher than women's. The remitted amount as a percentage of the income does not appear to be related to the fact that the sender has a bank account.

Great consideration should be given to the analysis of the cost. It is worth noticing that costs as reported in table 5.1 are only indicative of the user's perception of the cost for remittance services. World Bank experience shows that only the fee is generally perceived as a cost by the remittance sender. Other fundamental components of the cost are often not known by the sender or not considered as a part of the price that is being paid for the service. These components include the margin charged by the RSP on the exchange rate applied to the transaction, possible pick-up charge for the receiver, expenses to reach the disbursing location, work time spent to collect the money, and others. In particular, the exchange rate spread is generally applied and often not clearly disclosed by the RSP: this can be a very relevant component of the cost, in some cases even higher than the fee.

It is very interesting to compare the average cost as perceived by respondents to the survey with the findings of the World Bank Remittance Prices Worldwide database for the first quarter 2010 (see box 5.1). For the first time in February 2010, the Remittance Prices Worldwide database collected data for sending money from the Czech Republic to Ukraine. Significantly, the average fee of sending money from the Czech Republic to Ukraine through an MTO is 4.2 percent, which is very close to the total cost as perceived by migrants. In other words, this confirms that generally only the fee is perceived by migrants as a cost.

Table 5.1: Remitting amounts, costs, frequency

	China	Moldova	Mongolia	Poland	Russia	Slovak Republic	Ukraine	Vietnam	Total
Amount sent	1,426	428	300	336	200	286	200	548	353
Cost	15	14	11	14	9	0	6	16	9
% paid	1	3	4	3	4	0	3	3	3
Cost excluding free transactions	27	14	12	17	9	11	6	17	14
% paid excluding free transactions	2	4	4	5	4	2	3	3	4
Frequency (times/year)	2	3	6	8	4	6	6	2	5
Amount sent per year	3,000	1,520	1,600	2,733	1,200	2,558	1,200	1,500	1,808
Annual income	13,418	13,399	7,898	19,746	17,489	19,884	13,699	11,302	13,471
Percentage of annual income sent	30	12	22	17	7	12	9	11	13

All costs are indicated in U.S. dollars. Costs do not necessarily reflect the real price of sending money from the Czech Republic, but only the perception of the respondents to the survey, as generally users of remittance services are not aware of additional cost components, such as the margin applied on the exchange rate. Costs are also affected by transactions that do not have a cost (i.e., through friends or relatives); for this reason, figures excluding transactions at zero cost were also reported separately.

Box 5.1: Remittance prices worldwide

The World Bank **Remittance Prices Worldwide** database provides data on the cost of sending and receiving small amounts of money from one country to another.

Remittances are often initiated by migrant workers. The aggregate cash flows and the number of participants are enormous. The World Bank estimates that remittances totaled $420 billion in 2009, of which $317 billion went to developing countries, involving some 192 million migrants or 3 percent of world population. The money received is an important source of family and national income in many developing economies, representing in some cases a very relevant percentage of the GDP of the receiving countries.

The **Remittance Prices Worldwide** database covered 200 "country corridors" worldwide in the third quarter 2010. The corridors studied flow from 29 major remittance sending countries to 86 receiving countries, representing more than 60 percent of total remittances to developing countries.

The research and publication of remittance pricing worldwide serves four important purposes: benchmarking improvements, allowing comparisons among countries, supporting consumers' choices, and putting pressure on service providers to improve their services.

The **Remittance Prices Worldwide** database is available on the Internet at http://remittanceprices .worldbank.org

---

Anecdotal evidence collected by the World Bank, both during the survey and during the data collection for the Remittance Prices Worldwide database, suggests that in some cases RSPs in the Czech Republic might charge an exchange rate margin between two and four percent. If that was confirmed, the actual total cost for sending money would be between six and eight percent.

The Remittance Prices Worldwide database also confirms that sending money through banks from the Czech Republic to Ukraine is very expensive (between 8 and 36 percent) and transfers are slower compared to MTOs (from three to six days, compared to the same-day or instant services offered by MTOs at cheaper rates). The same price structure probably applies also to the other receiving countries surveyed.

Chinese and Vietnamese send higher amounts per transaction and only perform an average of two transactions per year: these two factors, along with others, contribute to the fact that sending money to China and Vietnam is relatively cheaper: respectively, two and three percent is the average cost that Chinese and Vietnamese migrants declare they pay, while the total average is above four percent. In the case of Ukraine, the low average cost can be explained by the preponderance of the market share that bus drivers seem to have: bus drivers usually deliver money to Ukraine for a flat fee of about USD 3.

Sending Methods and Market Structure

The Czech remittance market relies mostly on seven main MTOs, with nearly 1,300 collecting and disbursing points.[2] In 2008, there were 1,994 commercial bank branches in the Czech Republic: this represents a significant unused resource, as banks are almost absent from the remittance market. Česká Pošta, the national post service, has 3,372 offices and covers the vast majority of the national territory: also the post office network seems to be largely unused by migrants for sending remittances.

The scarce relevance of banks in the Czech remittance market is confirmed by the findings of the survey: less than 9 percent of respondents indicated that they use a bank to send money home. Friends or relatives travelling to the home country are the most used method of sending money from the Czech Republic, with over 30 percent of respondents preferring this method. MTOs follow with almost 28 percent of responses. A relevant flow of money is sent to neighbor countries by couriers, generally bus drivers. Surprisingly, notwithstanding its extensive network and the partnership with Western Union, the post office does not seem to be a major sending channel.

The use of friends or relatives to transfer money seems quite common for all nationalities surveyed. The use of this method is not related to the proximity of the receiving country, as Vietnamese, along with Ukrainians, are the ones using friends and relatives more often. On the contrary, proximity affects somewhat the use of couriers, as this response generally referred to bus drivers: for Ukraine and Moldova, couriers (i.e., bus drivers) are the most used transfer method. MTOs are present in all corridors with the only exception of the Slovak Republic, and dominate the market for remittances to Vietnam, Russia, and Mongolia. The only nationality for which banks play a major role is Polish; however, a significant portion of these transfers could be directed to the sender's bank account in Poland and used for bills or mortgage payments in the home country. In the case of China, a quite high value can be noticed for transfers through regular mail: this represents a specific service provided by the Czech Customs Post to send cash abroad by using special envelopes.

The case of the Slovak Republic is the most peculiar: as shown in table 5.2, the extent of usage of any formal[3] method is close to zero. The very high value for "other" in this case represents respondents who do not use any service to transfer money, but simply carry cash in their pocket when visiting their home country. For both cultural and historical reasons, Slovaks are the best integrated migrant community in the Czech Republic, at the point that they are generally not even perceived as foreigners by Czechs (many Slovaks are citizen or permanent residents in the Czech Republic). At the same time, Slovaks seem to keep a strong connection with their home country and their families residing in the Slovak Republic. It should also be considered that the Slovak Republic is quite close to Prague (only a few hours by train, bus, or car) and even closer to Brno, the second largest city of the Czech Republic. This allows Slovaks to visit relatively frequently (in general, every month) their country of origin and deliver money to their families in person.

When asked to name their preferred RSP, interviewees generally indicated an MTO (44 percent of cases). The low percentage of responses for friends or relatives in this case

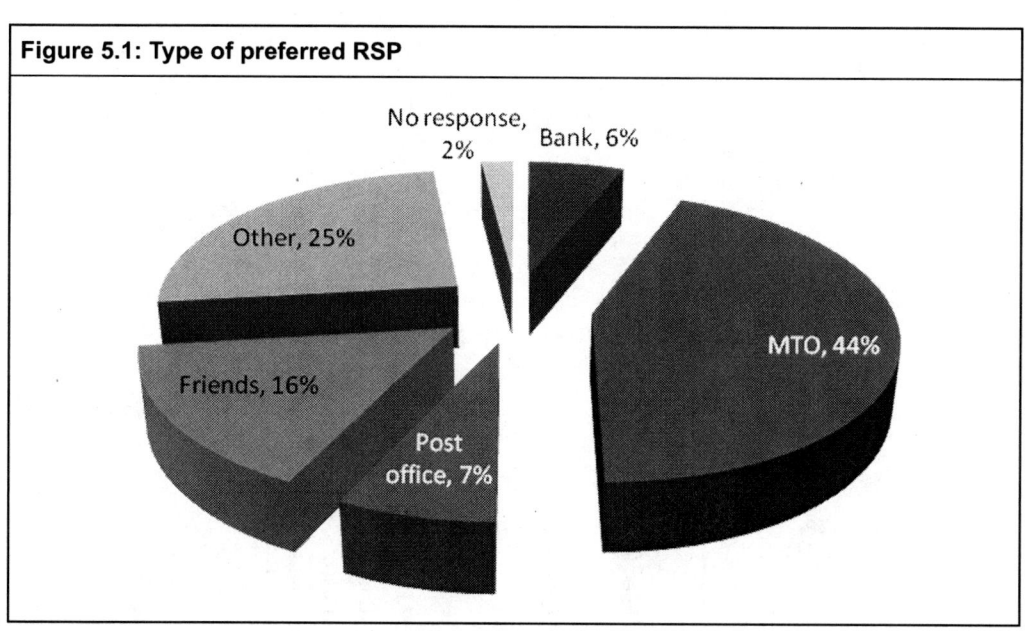

Figure 5.1: Type of preferred RSP

No response, 2%

Bank, 6%

Other, 25%

Friends, 16%

Post office, 7%

MTO, 44%

Table 5.2: Methods used by migrants to send money (%)

	China	Moldova	Mongolia	Poland	Russia	Slovak Rep.	Ukraine	Vietnam	Total
Friend/relative	36	25	21	29	30	28	40	39	**31**
MTO	26	18	42	11	44	0	25	47	**28**
Courier	0	31	1	11	10	7	32	0	**13**
Bank	15	10	11	31	6	1	0	1	**9**
Post office w/ West Union	5	4	6	9	5	0	0	1	**3**
Regular mail	19	0	0	2	0	0	0	0	**2**
ATM	0	8	0	0	3	0	0	0	**2**
Credit or debit cards	0	1	2	1	0	2	0	0	**1**
Post office w/ Other	0	1	1	4	0	0	0	0	**0**
Other	0	2	18	4	3	63	3	12	**12**

Table 5.3: Reasons for respondents' sending method choice

	China	Moldova	Mongolia	Poland	Russia	Slovak Republic	Ukraine	Vietnam	Total
Cost	11.6	24.1	20.3	19.4	18.1	33.2	23.2	11.4	**18.9**
Transfer speed	14.6	17.5	18.2	22.5	25.1	13.1	25.6	17.2	**18.8**
Safety	17.1	10.9	26.4	19.8	18.1	15.9	15.9	17.9	**17.7**
Easiness to use/understand	16.6	10.6	13.9	27.7	7.7	27.6	11.6	16.4	**16.3**
Convenience of receiving location	19.6	26.3	2.0	2.8	23.6	9.2	14.9	17.9	**15.1**
Convenience of sending location	15.7	9.5	7.1	6.7	6.6	0.7	8.5	19.0	**10.6**
Lack of official ID	0	0	0	0	0	0	0.3	0	**0**
Other	4.8	1.1	12.2	1.2	0.7	0.4	0	0.2	**2.5**

might be due to the fact that respondents would often not consider them as remittance service providers and that led them to indicate a company instead. The share for banks is confirmed to be very low, only six percent. The 25 percent of responses for "other" is differently composed depending on the nationality: in particular, bus drivers for Ukraine and Moldova and transfers performed by carrying cash for the Slovak Republic are the most relevant component for this category.

In most cases, the preferred RSP was Western Union, which is the favorite provider for 24 percent of respondents. In particular, Western Union seems to be very popular among Vietnamese, Russians, and Chinese. Friends or relatives account for 16 percent of responses, followed by Chequepoint (14 percent) and bus drivers (11 percent). Chequepoint is the favorite MTO for Ukrainians and Mongolians. Interestingly, Poles named a bank as their preferred RSP only in 18 percent of cases; however, when asked what methods they use for sending money, they indicated banks in more than 30 percent of answers (see table 5.2): this might be indicative of a low level of customer satisfaction.

Interviewees were asked to indicate the reasons of their RSP choice. Answers to this question do not allow for clear conclusions, as responses are quite evenly spread among the different options. However, a slightly stronger preference is expressed, overall, for cost and speed of transfer as factors influencing the choice (both around 19 percent). In particular, cost is the most relevant factor for Slovaks, and also very important for Moldovans. Ukrainians and Russians appear more concerned about the speed of the transfer. For Polish easiness to use the method play a critical role, while Mongolians are more worried about the safety of the transfer. Vietnamese expressed a slight preference for the convenience of the sending location. Finally, the convenience of the disbursing location for the receiver is a stronger element of the decision for the biggest receiving countries, China and Russia.

Migrants inform their decisions mostly through social networks (60 percent of responses, if other migrants, friends, families and word of mouth[4] are counted together). Recommendation from other migrants or friends is the source most frequently indicated as the one informing the sender's decision to use one provider (34 percent). Advertisements and means of communication are secondary to social networks in informing the interviewees' decision about what service to use for remitting money: advertisements in the street, newspapers, TV, radio, and leaflets all together account for about 35 percent of responses.

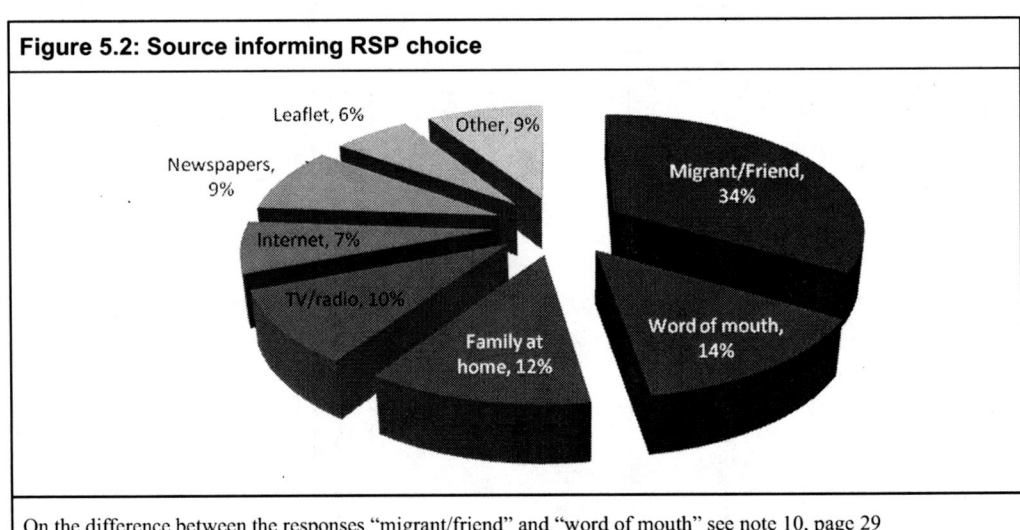

Figure 5.2: Source informing RSP choice

Leaflet, 6%
Other, 9%
Newspapers, 9%
Migrant/Friend, 34%
Internet, 7%
TV/radio, 10%
Family at home, 12%
Word of mouth, 14%

On the difference between the responses "migrant/friend" and "word of mouth" see note 10, page 29

Transparency

Remitters in the Czech Republic face several transparency obstacles when they receive information related to the transfer of their money.

Survey results show that remitters are attuned to the value of their money and find strategic ways to increase this value. One method used is the selection of the payout currency. In the majority of cases the U.S. dollar is the preferred currency to receive remittances. The next most preferred currency is the Euro, followed by the receiving country's currency and the Czech Koruna. Interestingly, almost all Ukrainians and Vietnamese responded that their transfers are paid to the receiver in U.S. dollars; since these transactions are generally also originated in U.S. dollars, this might be related to the fact that these are the biggest and best-established migrant communities in Prague, and migrants have easy access to alternative ways to exchange money at convenient rates before sending them home.

Results for Polish and Slovak migrants show different patterns. A little over half of Polish migrants prefer their home currency, while another 43 percent indicate the Czech Koruna. This may be due to the fact that it seems to be a common practice among Polish migrants to pay bills, mortgage, and similar expenses in their home country while living abroad. In the case of Slovaks, transfers are generally paid out in Euros, which became the official currency of the Slovak Republic in January 2009; this is a result of the fact that nearly all Slovaks carry cash while travelling to their home country and can easily change Czech Koruna to Euros in the Czech Republic.

In 84 percent of cases, no currency exchange occurs during the remittance transaction. This suggests that remitters exchange their money through other channels besides the RSPs. The most relevant exceptions are migrants from Poland, Vietnam, and Russia. Thus, collected data only allows an assessment of the transparency of the RSPs for these nationalities. While in the case of Russia it seems that RSPs generally disclose information concerning the exchange rate applied to the transaction, in the majority of cases Vietnamese and Polish migrants responded that the RSPs do not provide them with this information. It is worth noticing that Poles are the most relevant sample for this purpose, since most of them exchange Czech Koruna to Polish Zloty while remitting money to their home country.

Another index for the lack of transparency experienced by Vietnamese and Polish remitters is the fact that in most cases, when an exchange of currency occurs, the sender does not check by any means that the exchange declared by the RSP at the time of sending is the same actually applied at the time of withdrawal by the receiver.

Table 5.4: Currency in which transfers are paid (%)

	China	Moldova	Mongolia	Poland	Russia	Slovak Republic	Ukraine	Vietnam	Total
U.S. Dollar	50	51	86	0	75	0	98	95	**57**
Euro	44	42	10	4	5	94*	0	3	**25**
Receiving country currency	5	5	4	53	18	(94)*	0	2	**11**
Czech Koruna	0	1	0	43	0	6	0	0	**6**
Does not know	1	1	0	0	2	0	2	0	**1**

* The Euro became the official currency of the Slovak Republic in January 2009

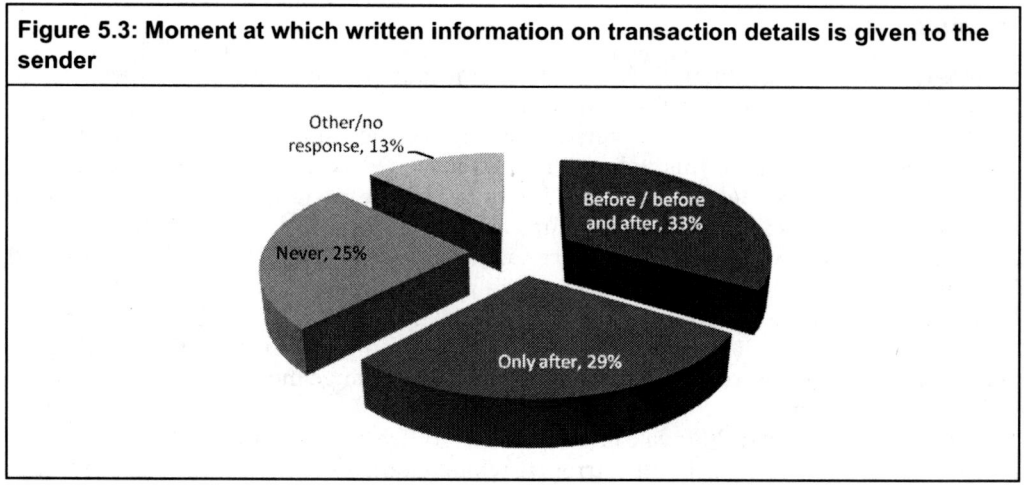

Figure 5.3: Moment at which written information on transaction details is given to the sender

Other/no response, 13%

Before / before and after, 33%

Never, 25%

Only after, 29%

The issue of transparency is further observed on the information received about the transaction. The survey reveals that one quarter of the sample receives written details on the transaction before it is executed, about one quarter receives them after the execution, and another quarter does not receive any written information about the transfer at all. Receiving written information after a transaction or not receiving it at all puts remitters and their families in a weak position, because they are less able to hold the RSP accountable for the service they provide.

Transfer Speed

As shown in table 5.5, remitters are generally given information on when the money sent will be available for the receiver's withdrawal, as only four percent of interviewees responded that they are not informed about the transfer speed or that this is uncertain. In most cases, senders are told that their transfer will take one day or less. A quarter of all senders are informed that their transfer will be ready for withdrawal within minutes. A comparison between transfer speed and cost paid for sending money confirms that the fastest transfers are also the most expensive.

Responses on transfer speed by sending method are displayed in table 5.6. Transfers through banks are generally very slow; most responses recorded under "other" indicate that bank transfers take several days. In nearly all cases, respondents who use MTOs or the Western Union service offered by the post office are told that their transfer will be available to the receiver instantly or within one day.

Table 5.5: Transfer speed and cost

Transfer Speed	% Responses	Average Amount Sent (USD)	Average Cost (%) [5]
Minutes	25	449	4.5
A couple of hours or first thing next morning	11	371	3
One day	24	200	3
I am not told how long, is uncertain	4	464	2
Other	23	566	2.5
Not applicable/does not know/no response	12	335	0

Table 5.6: Transfer speed by sending method

Speed	Bank	MTO	Post Office (Western Union)	Post Office (Other)	Regular Mail	Friends/ Relatives	Courier	ATM	Debit/ Credit Cards	Other
Minutes	25	47	64	0	7	20	6	67	30	12
Couple of hours or first thing next morning	4	16	17	13	0	10	8	0	0	8
One day	6	25	13	25	0	35	66	19	0	8
I am not told how long, is uncertain	3	1	0	0	0	7	7	0	10	2
Other	61	11	6	50	93	19	11	14	0	15
Not applicable/does not know/no response	1	0	0	12	0	9	2	0	60	55

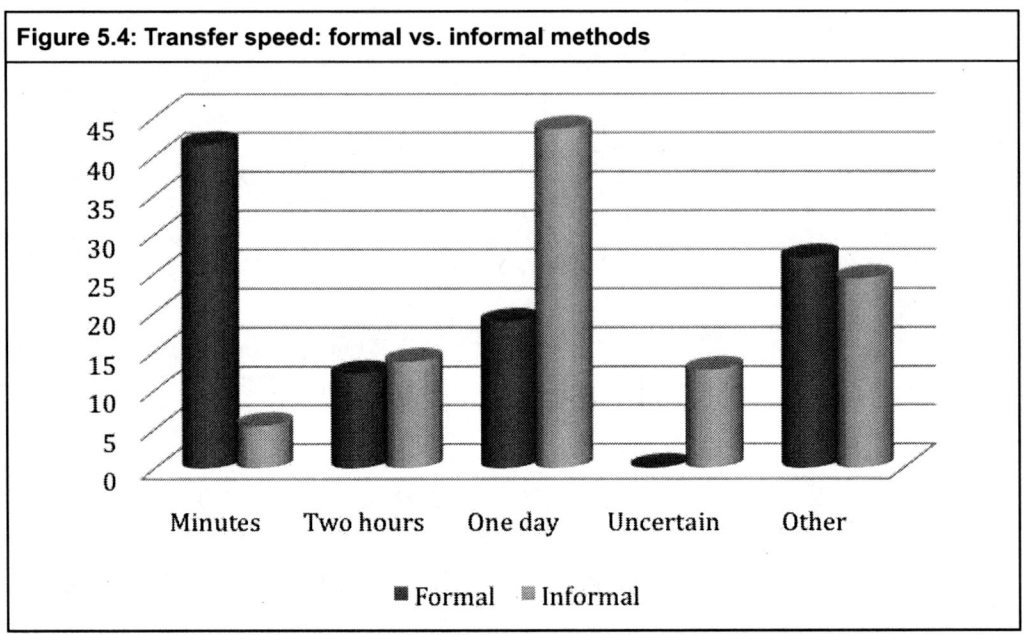

Figure 5.4: Transfer speed: formal vs. informal methods

Informal transfer methods, such as friends or relatives and bus drivers, are significantly slower than formal means, such as MTOs. As shown in figure 5.4, transfers through informal methods take generally one day, while in the formal market, remitters are usually informed that the money will be available for the receiver within minutes. Additionally, the percentage of uncertainty, almost zero in the formal market, is close to 13 percent when informal methods are used.

Methods of Collection

According to survey results, the most common way to collect the money is by visiting one of the branches of the RSP in the receiving country. In fact, in 39 percent of cases money is collected by visiting either any or a specific branch of the RSP. Having the money delivered directly to the receiver's house accounts for 34 percent of responses. In nearly half of these cases, the preferred method used is friends or relatives travelling to the home country. On the other hand, when the transfer method is an MTO, recipients generally visit a branch in order to withdraw the money.

When looking at the data from a receiving country perspective, a few peculiarities can be observed. In the Slovak Republic, nearly everyone has the money delivered directly to their home, due to the fact that most transfers are made by simply carrying the money when visiting the home country, or through friends or relatives. On the contrary, in the case of Mongolia, very few people have the transfer delivered directly to their home, and the most common collection method is visiting a specific branch of the RSP. In this case, the prevalence of this option over the possibility of visiting any branch is due to the fact that RSPs often have only one disbursing point in the receiving city. China is the only country where collecting money at the post office is a commonly used option; this relates to the fact that over 18 percent of migrants use regular mail to send money home. Similarly, Poles are the only nationality receiving money in their bank account and, at the same time, the only migrant community where banks represent a significant share of the market. Withdrawing money from an ATM is a relevant collection method only in Moldova.

Table 5.7: Collection methods

	China	Moldova	Mongolia	Poland	Russia	Slovak Rep.	Ukraine	Vietnam	Total
It is delivered to their home	23	22	4	29	30	91	41	33	**34**
Going to any branch of a bank/MTO	43	21	23	16	20	0	5	38	**20**
Withdrawal at a specific bank/MTO	0	9	66	7	32	0	21	13	**19**
Other	0	33	7	11	13	9	33	14	**16**
They go to the post office	34	2	0	9	0	0	0	1	**5**
Collect the money in their bank account	0	2	0	27	3	0	0	1	**4**
Withdrawal from an ATM	0	11	0	1	2	0	0	0	**2**

Problems Encountered in Remitting

In the large majority of cases, respondents never experienced mishaps when sending money home; only 16 percent of interviewees reported some kind of problem. The most common issue is related to the speed of the transfer (money were delivered with a relevant delay), while the other types of issues recurred in less than two percent of cases.

When aggregated by preferred transfer method, data show that banks and couriers rate slightly below the average, with about 22 percent of respondents declaring they had a problem in the past. Evidence seems to indicate the least reliable method be the service provided by Western Union through the post office, which accounts for 30 percent of customers who experienced some kind of problem while using this service. It is worth noticing that informal methods seem to be slightly more reliable, as 87 percent of interviewees never had a problem versus the 84 percent for formal channels.

Chinese more often experienced loss of the sums sent (almost 4 percent of responses), probably due to the fact that they are also the only ones using regular mail for sending money. Chinese migrants also experienced mistakes on the receiver's name, due to the fact that first and last name can easily be confused by the RSP's agent. Receiving an incorrect amount seems to be an issue only for Polish migrants (more than 5 percent). Interestingly, Ukrainians and Moldovans show the highest percentage of cases where the receiver had to pay a fee to withdraw the money. This should be related to the wide use of bus drivers to deliver money for these two nationalities and to the fact that asking the receiver to pay a fee upon delivery could be a common practice for this method.

In case of problems, the interviewees generally contacted, or would contact, the provider of the remittance service, whether MTO, bank, or post office. It is important to notice that the general prosecutor and financial arbiter are never contacted by migrants, who are probably not even aware of the availability of these options. A high percentage of responses for "friends" have been recorded: this should not be interpreted in the sense that the sender would seek friends' help; it is instead due to the fact that the sender would usually contact a friend when the same friend was being used to transfer the money. Finally, Slovaks resort in a relatively high percentage to the police, since they generally carry money while travelling to the Slovak Republic and the only problem they are likely to experience is being robbed.

Preference for Change

More than half of the interviewees would switch to a more efficient way to send money home. Migrants seem to be more interested in banking services, such as direct deposit on bank account, rather than in innovative payment services, such as cards, the Internet, or

Table 5.8: Problems associated with preferred methods of money transfer

Problem	MTO	Bank	Post Office with Western Union	Regular Mail	Friends or Relatives	Courier	Other	Total
No problem	83.3	78.0	70.2	86.7	85.7	78.9	88.0	**83.7**
Days of delay	11.4	12.6	17.0	3.3	8.9	13.7	4.9	**9.6**
Fee	0.3	1.6	2.1	0	2.6	5.0	2.2	**1.7**
Money lost	0.8	0.8	0	10.0	0.5	0	2.2	**1.3**
Sum incorrect	0.8	1.6	4.3	0	0.7	1.9	1.6	**1.2**
Other	3.5	5.5	6.4	0	1.6	0.6	1.1	**2.5**

Table 5.9: Preference to use a more efficient way to send remittances

	China	Moldova	Mongolia	Poland	Russia	Slovak Republic	Ukraine	Vietnam	Total
Would not change	15.5	72.7	13.4	33.6	45.5	40.0	52.7	49.1	**40.2**
Direct deposit on bank account	71.8	18.2	51.8	21.8	29.1	0	3.6	31.8	**28.6**
Internet	6.4	0.9	10.7	31.8	17.3	24.5	7.3	1.8	**12.6**
Mobile phone	1.8	0	9.8	2.7	3.6	16.4	4.5	0.9	**5.0**
Remittance card	0	0.9	11.6	9.1	0	0	2.7	6.4	**3.9**
Other	2.7	3.6	2.7	0.9	0	0	0	9.1	**2.4**
Does not know/no response	1.8	3.6	0	0	4.5	19.1	29.1	0.9	**7.4**

Table 5.10: Preference for change by past experiences

		Had A Problem	
		Yes	**No**
Wants to change	*Yes*	63	56
	No	37	44

mobile-based solutions. This trend is particularly evident among Asian migrants, while Poles and Slovaks show a stronger preference for Internet services. In particular, it is worth noticing that Slovaks show no interest at all in direct deposits, and a similar trend can be observed among Ukrainians.

Data confirm the intuitive assumption that those who experienced problems are more willing to change their method of transferring money (63 percent). Even though a strong relation between these two factors is predictable, it is worth noticing that 56 percent of those who never experienced problems expressed their preference for change, leading to the conclusion that other elements, such as cost and speed, influence the preference for change.

There is a positive relation between the amount remitted and the preference for change: migrants who are open to change send more than those who are not interested in a different service. Significantly, those who would rather remit through direct deposit to bank account are those who send the largest average amount (over USD 1,200).

Notes

[1] There are several possible explanations for this: it seems that for cultural reasons Chinese are not comfortable about disclosing their annual income; also, most Chinese migrants in Prague own restaurants or stores (retail or wholesale), and on the one hand, they declare that it is hard for them to estimate an annual income, while on the other hand, they might be concerned about fiscal implications of disclosing this information.

[2] Inter-American Dialogue, October 2009.

[3] The distinction between the *formal* and *informal* sector for remittance services is controversial. From a payment-system perspective, it is not particularly relevant whether a payment instrument is formal or informal, nor is there a presumption that the formal sector is preferable to the informal one. Additionally, it is worth noticing that the distinction between formal and informal is not used in the GPs (see CPSS—World Bank "General Principles for International Remittance Services," box 2, page 7). For the purpose of this report, the distinction between formal and informal is used only with the objective of isolating data that concern RSPs (i.e., entities, operating as businesses, that provide remittance services for a price to end users, either directly or through agents) from other methods of sending money (i.e., friends, relatives, or the sender himself carrying cash while travelling to the home country, or use of regular mail or couriers for sending cash).

[4] The response *word of mouth* refers to generic information that the respondent heard somewhere or from someone he or she would not be able to specify. The responses *migrants or friends* and *family at home* refer to a specific suggestion that the sender was given by a friend or a relative. The response *word of mouth* is often considered an indicator for the effectiveness of marketing techniques, while the answers for friends or relatives could be considered a result of direct experience. However, it is worth noticing that the difference between these two responses is quite subtle and sometime not easy to explain, especially in the short timeframe of the interview.

[5] As explained on page 10, costs are only indicative of the migrants' perception of the price and may not reflect the actual cost of the transaction, due to the fact that some components of the cost, such as exchange rate applied, are generally hidden or not perceived as actual costs by users.

CHAPTER 6

Main Conclusions

This section provides a series of conclusions drawn from the analysis of the above outcomes. Observations are based on the General Principles for International Remittance Services (GPs).[1] In particular, the main focus is on:

- Transparency and consumer protection (GP1)
- Payment system infrastructure (GP2)
- Market structure and competition (GP4)

General Principles for International Remittance Services and Related Roles

Transparency and consumer protection
General Principle 1. The market for remittance services should be transparent and have adequate consumer protection.

Payment system infrastructure
General Principle 2. Improvements to payment system infrastructure that have the potential to increase the efficiency of remittance services should be encouraged.

Legal and regulatory framework
General Principle 3. Remittance services should be supported by a sound, predictable, non-discriminatory, and proportionate legal and regulatory framework in relevant jurisdictions.

Market structure and competition
General Principle 4. Competitive market conditions, including appropriate access to domestic payments infrastructures, should be fostered in the remittance industry.

Governance and risk management
General Principle 5. Remittance services should be supported by appropriate governance and risk management practices.

Roles of remittance service providers and public authorities
A. *The role of remittance service providers.* Remittance service providers should participate actively in the implementation of the GPs.

B. *The role of public authorities.* Public authorities should evaluate what action to take to achieve the public policy objectives through implemenation of the GPs.

Transparency and Consumer Protection

Transparency and adequate consumer protection are essential elements to achieve a reliable and competitive market for remittances.

Transparency about prices and service features is crucial for the consumers to make informed choices between different services and for the creation of a competitive market. RSPs should therefore provide such information in easily accessible and understandable way. As far as possible, such information should include at least: (i) the total price (i.e., fees

---

Box 6.1: Transparency to the sender

When a customer inquires about a specific remittance transfer, full transparency would mean that RSPs clearly disclosed the following information without requiring any other action from the consumer such as opening an account or committing to use the remittance service:

- ▦   The total amount in originating currency that will be paid by the sender
- ▦   The amount in disbursing currency that will be paid to the final recipient
- ▦   The fees paid by both sender and receiver (and any other relevant costs such as taxes) and the exchange rate
- ▦   The time when the remittance will be available for pick-up by the recipient or delivered to the recipient
- ▦   The location(s) where the remittance will be available for pick-up

If the above information varies according to how the receiver is paid or according to the information the receiver is able to provide about the sender, this should be clear to the sender.

For key remittance corridors, it may be appropriate to provide the information in the languages of both the sending and receiving countries.

If the customer chooses to use the remittance service, the RSP should also provide the information above (plus the information provided by the sender to identify the receiver) in written form as confirmation of the agreed service.

To achieve full transparency, RSPs should also provide information on any other relevant aspects of their service.

Source: CPSS-WB, General principles for international remittance services, box 6, page 31

---

at both ends of the transaction, foreign exchange rate applied, and other possible costs to the user), (ii) the time it will take for the funds to reach the receiver, and (iii) the specific locations of the RSP access points in both sending and receiving countries. It should also be clear to the sender whether the price or other aspects of the service vary according to, for example, how the receiver is paid (e.g., in cash or by crediting an account) or the ability of the sender to provide information about the sender (e.g., relevant account number and bank identifier).

Appropriate consumer protection is also important. Senders should be provided with adequate rights as consumers of remittance services, including error-resolution administrative procedures. Although many countries have in place mechanisms for the resolution of domestic consumer disputes, the cross-border nature of remittances and cultural and language barriers can make such procedures byzantine for migrants.

The survey highlights a series of factors showing a low level of transparency and consumer protection in the Czech remittance market. This conclusion can be drawn through: (a) the analysis of senders' perception of the costs; (b) the low level of information and awareness around the currency exchange aspects of the transaction; (c) the RSPs' level of information disclosure; (d) the reaction to problems.

As described in Chapter 5, interviewed migrants generally perceive the fee as the only cost associated to the remittance service. However, the total price of the transaction also depends on the exchange rate applied[2] (when the two legs of the transaction are executed in different currencies) and, possibly, on the fee charged to the receiver by the disbursing RSP or its agent. Therefore, to know the total price of the transfer, the sender needs to be informed about all of the above elements.

Survey results also show that often users of remittance services in the Czech Republic are not given written information on the details of the transfer. The large use of informal channels certainly affects this figure. However, this constitutes one more element indicating a lack of transparency in the market.

It is not clear to remitters what tools they can use to protect their interests in case of problems when transferring money. Nearly all conflicts are handled within the relation between the RSP and its client, and the only authority migrants refer to is the police. No other mechanism for the resolution of disputes is used. In particular, as noted above, migrants never indicated that they contacted the general prosecutor or the Financial Arbiter. In particular, considering the nature of remittance transactions, the Financial Arbiter could represent the ideal institution for customers to refer to in case of controversies with RSPs.

A number of possible actions have been identified to improve transparency and consumer protection in the market for remittance services. On the one hand, RSPs could put a greater effort toward disclosing all the relevant information to their customers at the moment of the transaction (see box 6.2). On the other hand, initiatives can be undertaken by national authorities, such as publication of comparative information on the prices for remittance services, financial literacy campaigns, or reforms of the framework for customer protection.

One of the most efficient means to improve the transparency of the market for remittances that has been identified is the creation of publicly available databases containing detailed information on the cost of remitting from or to a single country. Price-comparison tables enable remitters to assess at a glance how much their beneficiaries will receive, taking into account both commission charged and exchange rate applied. An increased level of transparency can effectively drive down the cost of sending remittances.

Financial literacy programs would inform migrant workers about their rights in the area of remittances, and of the benefits of the various different payment and banking options available. This would bring profit both to the general economic environment and to the private sector, as consumers would be able to increase their understanding of other financial services, thereby making them potential and consistent users of such services.

With regard to customer protection, specific conflict-resolution schemes could be adopted, and a set of clear, publicly available, easily applicable procedures in cases of fraud and disputes could be put in place. Fraud and dispute-resolution procedures should recognize that migrants may face particular difficulties in enforcing their rights through the general legal system, and the peculiarities of remitters should be carefully taken into account (e.g., language, culture, and business hours).

The powers of the Financial Arbiter to create effective mechanisms for the resolution of consumer complaints in the case of fraud or disputes are currently very limited in the Czech Republic. The scope of its jurisdiction could be extended to all payments, no matter their destination or origin. Remittances could also be explicitly mentioned among those financial services covered by the protection of this institution.

Payment System Infrastructure

Remittance services, except perhaps those that are entirely cash-based, depend at some stage on the domestic payments infrastructure for settlement and, sometimes, also for the transfer of information. RSPs can often make better use of the payments infrastructure that has been developed, through greater standardization of payment instruments, more automation of their processing, and increased interoperability of the associated networks.

The payment systems infrastructure of the Czech Republic is well developed, and remittances collecting points are widely available. MTOs count on an extensive network of agencies, particularly in the areas where migrants live. Banks also have a relevant and widespread presence all over the country. Credit unions and a considerable number of foreign exchange entities, whose branches are often used by MTOs as collecting and disbursing agencies, operate in the country.

Conclusions on the payment system infrastructure can only be indirectly drawn, since the survey focused exclusively on the demand side. **However, two main findings can be extracted from the migrants' answers: (a) banks and post offices represent a significant resource that is largely unused for remittance services; (b) improvements of the infrastructure for cross-border payments could help reduce the use of inefficient means for sending money abroad, such as carrying cash when travelling and other informal channels.**

Banks have both a limited comprehension of the real scale of the remittance market in the Czech Republic and a business philosophy that does not consider migrants as potentially profitable customers. In the rare cases when banks are aware of the phenomenon, their internal procedures have not been adapted to offer a customized service to migrants, nor have they created new external channels or products to attract these customers.

Correspondent relationships can be instrumental to providing access to remitters' relatives abroad via bank accounts. Banks in the Czech Republic are not promoting the use of electronic methods to send remittances, for example through the creation of correspondent relationships with other banks in the receiving country. This is mainly due to the fact that the costs to set up an adequate cross-border infrastructure would not be immediately and fully counterbalanced by a critical mass of transactions large enough to repay the initial investments.

Payment system infrastructure links with the major countries of destination of migrants' remittances might be a tool to increase the efficiency of these services. This instrument, already in use in major corridors such as USA–Mexico, could be suitable for the Czech Republic. The main benefit of clearing applications such as an ACH would be to facilitate the interconnections with other similar systems abroad. Banks would benefit from standardized processes and common efficient distribution channels, considerably reducing the costs of sending money abroad.

Česká Pošta, the national postal service, has an extensive network in the country and offers different products for sending money abroad. However, **the post office network[3] is definitely not used to its full potential.** Along with marketing initiatives and actions aimed at better serving migrants, an overall reform of the national postal service, including the modernization of its telecommunication infrastructure and the innovation of operating procedures, would certainly increase the role of Česká Pošta and positively affect the market for remittances in the country. In particular, interconnections and agreements on common standards and procedures between Česká Pošta and the national postal services of the countries of origin of the main migrant communities could lead to the creation of preferential channels for remittances.

Market Structure and Competition

The efficiency of remittance services depends on there being a competitive business environment. Competitive markets can help limit monopolistic practices and lead to lower prices and improved service levels. In some places, or for certain remittance corridors, the demand for remittance services may be insufficient to support multiple RSPs, but even in this case, provided that the market is contestable—without barriers to entry—the benefits of competition should be felt. Competition can be assisted by discouraging RSPs from imposing exclusivity conditions on agents.

Survey results confirm the common belief that there is a low level of competition in the market for remittance services in the Czech Republic. Some RSPs clearly occupy a position of supremacy in the market. The scarce relevance of important players such as banks and the post office is not favoring competition in the market. Moreover, the wide use by senders of informal means for transferring money abroad, such as through friends or relatives or by carrying cash while travelling, makes the market less attractive for RSPs.

The analysis of the survey's outcomes suggests that cost is an important component for migrants' choice of a sending method. The low cost is generally the reason why migrants prefer methods that are not efficient and, to some extent, not safe. However, the senders' decision is strongly affected also by other factors; in particular the speed of the transfer and its safeness. Thus, efficient instruments to send money would have a great potential for gaining more relevant market shares, if offered at lower cost. This finding should stimulate the efforts of the market players toward a reduction of costs to acquire new customers, especially among the migrants who are currently not using any institutional way to send money to their home country. Moreover, a competitive market would force RSPs to lower costs, and more migrants could enter the market, attracted by efficient services at lower costs.

The survey's findings should be particularly relevant for banks. As noted in Chapter 5, remittance senders showed a clear interest for banks' services, in particular direct deposits to the receiver's bank account. Customers are obviously restrained from using banks to transfer money by the very high prices and slowness of the transfer, and by the fact that banks are generally not ready to welcome remittance users (e.g., banks do not offer specific services for migrants and do not usually provide forms and conditions in multiple languages).

Notes

[1] The World Bank and the CPSS co-chaired a task force to establish general principles of universal applicability that identify the features and functions that should be satisfied by remittance systems, providers, and financial intermediaries. Published in January 2007, the General Principles for International Remittance Services provide the first internationally recognized payment system framework for remittance transfers. The General Principles are aimed at the public policy objectives of achieving safe and efficient international remittance services. To this end, the market for the services should be contestable, transparent, accessible, and sound.

[2] RSPs typically charge senders an exchange rate that includes a margin above the current interbank or wholesale market rate. The margin is essentially another form of fee, not easy to calculate for the sender, who is unlikely to know what the current interbank market rate is.

[3] In an increasing number of countries, the post office network is expanding its potential in the collection of remittances, and the Universal Postal Union is implementing several projects around the world to make use of this often under-evaluated network.

Possible Key Actions

In conclusion, the following items requiring action by national authorities and RSPs can be identified.

- The survey highlights a series of factors showing a low level of transparency and consumer protection in the Czech remittance market. These issues should be addressed by both the authorities and the RSPs. Authorities could consider undertaking several actions, such as the creation of a national database for remittance prices, the organization of financial literacy campaigns, and the reform of the framework for consumer protection. On the other hand, RSPs could provide their customers with a more complete set of information and do so in writing; a common reference exchange rate to be used as a basis for calculating the price of the remittance service could also be agreed by the industry.

- Improvements of the infrastructure for cross-border payments could help reduce the use of inefficient means for sending money abroad. Payment system infrastructure links with the major countries of destination of migrants' remittances might be a useful tool to increase the efficiency of these services.

- The lack of competition represents one of the main constraints for the development of an efficient market for remittance services in the Czech Republic. In order to increase competition, banks should be encouraged to enter the market for remittances by offering specific services for migrants. The remittance services offered by the post office should be better promoted, and migrants should be better served, in order to open to the market the extensive network already available.

- The average cost for sending money from the Czech Republic to the country of origins of migrants is high, and the reduction of prices for remittance services should be considered an objective by the authorities.

The Questionnaire

IMPLEMENTING THE CPSS-WB GENERAL PRINCIPLES
FOR INTERNATIONAL REMITTANCE SERVICES

WORLD BANK

Questionnaire for the Czech National Survey on the Market for Remittances

MINISTRY OF FINANCE
OF THE CZECH REPUBLIC

July–September 2009

Good morning/afternoon. We are conducting a survey on remittances in order to find solutions for migrants in the Czech Republic and we are interested in your opinion. The survey is completely anonymous and will only take 15 minutes of your time.

Questionnaire number _____

Interviewer _____

Location _____

Date _____

A) To begin, do you send remittances? *(MARK ONLY ONE)*

YES		1
NO *(DISCONTINUE SURVEY)*		0

1) What country are you from? *(MARK ONLY ONE)*

Ukraine		1
Vietnam		2
Slovak Republic		3
Russia		4
China		5
Moldova		6
Mongolia		7
Poland		8
Other *(DISCONTINUE SURVEY)*		0

A. REMITTANCES

2) To what city do you send money usually? *(ENTER ONLY ONE)*

_____		
Does not know/No response		99

3) On average, how much money do you send each time? *(ENTER ONLY ONE)*

a. AMOUNT _____ b. CURRENCY (CZK, USD, EUR, ETC.) _____		
Does not know/No response		99

4) How frequently do you send money during a year?

_____ TIMES		
Does not know/No response		99

5) How much do you pay on average to send the money?

a. AMOUNT _____ **b.** CURRENCY (*USE SAME AS IN Q3*) _____		
Does not know/No response		99

6) Do you specify the transfer to be paid in Euros, Dollars or in your country's currency? (*MARK ONLY ONE*)

Euro		1
Dollar		2
Home country currency		3
Does not know/No response		99

If response is same currency as in Q3, skip to Q7; if different, skip to Q6.1

6.1) Do you know whether an exchange rate is applied to the transaction?
(*MARK ONLY ONE*)

YES		1
NO		0
Does not know/No response		99

6.2) How does the remittance company make you aware of the exchange rate?
(*MARK ONLY ONE*)

I am not made aware, I don't have a way of knowing until after the transaction is made		1
I am not made aware, I have to ask at the transfer location		2
I am told when am making the transaction		3
I am told when I call over the phone prior to going to the location		4
There are posted signs at the location showing the exchange rate of the day		5
Other (**i.** please specify: _____)		6
Does not know/No response		99

6.3) How do you confirm that the reported exchange rate is the same as at the time of cash withdrawal? (*MARK ONLY ONE*)

I do not confirm the exchange rate, I trust it is right		1
I give the exchange rate information to my relative and he/she confirms it to me		2
My relative asks me about the exchange rate and I confirm whether that was the amount paid		3
Other (**i.** please specify: _____)		4
Does not know/No response		99

7) The written information about the details of the transfer, is given to you *(MARK ONLY ONE)*

Before the transaction is completed	1
After the transaction is completed	2
Before and after the transaction is completed	3
I do not receive written information about the details of the transaction	4
Does not know/No response	99

8) Which is your preferred method of sending money home? *(MARK ALL THAT APPLY)*

a.	Bank/Credit Union	1
b.	Money Transfer Operator (Western Union, Exchange Bureaus, etc.)	1
c.	Post Office with Western Union	1
d.	Post Office with Other	1
e.	Regular mail	1
f.	Friends/Relatives traveling	1
g.	Courier	1
h.	ATM	1
i.	Debit/Credit Cards	1
j.	Mobile Phone	1
k.	Other (i. like a super market, please specify: _____)	1
	Does not know/No response	99

9) What is the name of your preferred remittance company (not method)? *(ENTER ONLY ONE)*

_____	
Does not know/No response	99

10) Why do you send money with these methods? *(MARK ALL THAT APPLY)*

a.	It is inexpensive compared to other companies and methods	1
b.	It is fast	1
c.	It is easy to use/comprehensible	1
d.	It is safe	1
e.	It is close to where I live	1
f.	It is conveniently located for the people I send the money to	1
g.	I have no official ID/Passport	1
h.	Other (i. please specify: _____)	1
	Does not know/No response	99

11) **What source most informs your decision to choose a remittance company?**
(MARK ALL THAT APPLY)

a.	Recommendation from other immigrants or friends		1
b.	Word of mouth		1
c.	Advertisement in the streets		1
d.	Advertisement in the newspaper		1
e.	Advertisement on the TV/Radio		1
f.	Advertisement on a leaflet in my native language		1
g.	The embassy/consulate gave me the information		1
h.	Internet		1
i.	My family at home gave me the information		1
j.	During a meeting of the migrant association I am a member of		1
k.	During the mass/in the church		1
l.	Other (**i.** please specify:_____)		1
	Does not know/No response		99

12) **How long are you told at your most used remittance company that it takes for the transfer to be ready for withdrawal?** *(MARK ONLY ONE)*

Minutes		1
A couple of hours or first thing next morning		2
One day		3
I am not told how long, is uncertain		4
Other (**i.** please specify:_____)		5
Does not know/No response		99

13) **How do the receivers usually collect the money?** *(MARK ALL THAT APPLY)*

a.	They withdraw the money at a specific bank/Money Transfer Operator		1
b.	They go to any branch of a bank/Money Transfer Operator		1
c.	They receive it in their bank account		1
d.	They withdraw the money at an ATM		1
e.	It is delivered to their home		1
f.	They go to the Post Office		1
g.	They receive it in their mobile phone account		1
h.	Other (**i.** please specify:_____)		1
	Does not know/No response		99

14) When the receivers collect the money . . . *(MARK ONLY ONE)*

Their only choice is to receive in local currency	1
They have a choice to receive in local currency or foreign currency (CZK, USD, EUR, etc)	2
Does not know/No response	99

15) Have you ever had problems in the past when you have sent the money? *(MARK ALL THAT APPLY)*

a.	The money was not received, and I lost everything	1
b.	The sum received was not correct	1
c.	The money arrived with many days of delay	1
d.	The receiver had to pay a fee to withdraw the money	1
e.	Other (**i.** please specify: _____)	1
f.	I never had any problem	1
	Does not know/No response	99

If marked yes for Q15f or marked Does not know/No response, skip to Q17. Otherwise, ask Q16.

16) In case of any problem during the sending of your money, which of the following authorities/persons have you contacted/would you contact to request help? *(MARK ALL THAT APPLY)*

a.	The police	1
b.	The general prosecutor	1
c.	The Financial Arbiter	1
d.	The embassy/consulate	1
e.	The management of the agency you send money to	1
f.	The manager of the Money Transfer Operator	1
g.	The director of the Bank/Post Office	1
h.	Friends	1
i.	None of above	1
j.	Other (**i.** please specify:_____)	1
	Does not know/No response	99

17) Would you like to use a more efficient way to send your remittance? *(MARK ONLY ONE)*

Remittance card		1
Direct deposit on a bank account		2
Internet		3
Mobile phone based transfers		4
Other (**i.** please specify: _____)		5
I won't change		0
Does not know/No response		99

B. FINANCIAL SERVICES

18) Do you have a bank account? *(MARK ONLY ONE)*

Checking account		1
Savings account		2
Both		3
Neither		0
Does not know/No response		99

19) Do you have a mobile phone? *(MARK ONLY ONE)*

Yes		1
No		0
Does not know/No response		99

C. DEMOGRAPHICS

20) What is your sex? *(DO NOT ACTUALLY ASK! MARK ONLY ONE)*

Male		1	Female		0

21) How old are you?

_____ YEARS		Does not know/No response		99

22) For how long have you been living in the Czech Republic?

_____ YEARS		Does not know/No response		99

23) What type of work do you currently do in the Czech Republic? *(MARK ONLY ONE)*

Enterpriser	100
Employee	101
Housewife	102
Student/Retired	103
Unemployed	104
Other (i. please specify: _____)	105
Does not know/No response	999

24) In which sector? *(MARK ONLY ONE)*

Agriculture, forestry and fishing	200
Manufacturing and other industry	201
Construction	202
Wholesale and retail trade	203
Transportation and storage	204
Accommodation and food service activities	205
Information and communications	206
Financial and insurance	207
Real estate activities	208
Professional, scientific and technical	209
Administrative and support services	210
Public administration	211
Education	212
Human health and social work activities	213
Arts entertainment and recreation	214
Other (i. please specify: _____)	215
Does not know/No response	999

25) More or less, how much is your salary here in the Czech Republic per month?

_____ CZK	
Does not know/No response	99

26) What is your legal status in the Czech Republic? *(MARK ONLY ONE)*

Citizen		1
Legal Resident (living in the Czech Republic for more than 12 months)		2
Temporary Resident (living in the Czech Republic for less than 12 months)		3
Refugee		4
Illegal resident		5
Does not know/No response		99

Tables of Responses

Amount, cost, frequency, and income (Questions 3, 4, 5, 25)

	China	Moldova	Mongolia	Poland	Russian Federation	Slovak Republic	Ukraine	Vietnam	All
Average amount sent per transaction(USD)	2,715.4	549.5	336.9	615.1	397.0	393.3	200.5	921.4	765.2
Average cost (USD)	28.6	17.0	15.7	12.2	12.1	0.9	5.6	20.9	13.8
Average cost (%)	1	4	5	4	4	-	3	3	3
Annual frequency	3.1	4.0	6.7	7.9	4.8	8.3	7.7	3.1	5.7
Average amount sent per year (USD)	5,694.9	1,872.1	2,293.7	3,962.9	1,488.1	2,895.1	1,419.1	2,423.3	2,756.2
Annual income (USD)	12,980.4	14,994.9	8,066.0	20,873.3	17,730.8	20,896.7	14,503.6	13,559.6	15,105.2
Average amount sent per year as a percentage of annual income(%)	39	15	30	19	8	14	10	13	19

Do you specify the transfer to be paid in Euro, USD, Czech Koruna, or in your country's currency? (Question 6)

	China	Moldova	Mongolia	Poland	Russian Federation	Slovak Republic	Ukraine	Vietnam	All
Euro	44.5	41.8	9.8	3.6	5.5	93.6	-	2.7	25.2
USD	50.0	50.9	85.7	-	75.5	-	98.2	95.5	57.0
Receiving country currency	4.5	5.5	4.5	52.7	18.2	-	-	1.8	10.9
Czech Koruna	-	0.9	-	42.7	-	6.4	-	-	6.2
does not know/no response	0.9	0.9	-	0.9	0.9	-	1.8	-	0.7

Do you know whether an exchange rate is applied to the transaction? (Question 6.1)

	China	Moldova	Mongolia	Poland	Russian Federation	Slovak Republic	Ukraine	Vietnam	All
NO	-	0.9	2.7	1.8	-	-	-	0.9	0.8
YES	4.5	11.8	1.8	49.1	25.5	-	-	29.1	15.2
does not know/no response	95.4	87.3	95.5	49.1	74.5	100.0	100.0	70.0	84.0

How does the remittance company make you aware of the exchange rate? (Question 6.2)

	China	Moldova	Mongolia	Poland	Russian Federation	Slovak Republic	Ukraine	Ukraine	Vietnam	All
I am not made aware	0.0	1.8	2.7	11.8	0.9	0.0	0.0	0.0	2.2	0.0
I am not made aware, unless I ask	0.9	0.0	0.0	16.4	0.0	0.0	0.0	25.5	5.3	0.9
I am told when making the transaction	1.8	5.5	0.9	14.5	9.1	0.0	0.0	4.5	4.5	1.8
I am told when I call over the phone before reaching the location	0.9	1.8	0.0	0.9	9.1	0.0	0.0	0.0	1.6	0.9
There are posted signs at the location showing the exchange rate	0.9	1.8	0.0	8.2	2.7	0.0	0.0	0.0	1.7	0.9
Other	0.0	0.9	0.9	0.9	3.6	0.0	0.0	0.9	0.9	0.0
does not know/no response	95.4	88.2	95.5	47.3	74.5	100	100	69.1	83.8	95.4

How do you confirm that the reported exchange rate is the same as at the time of cash withdrawal? (Question 6.3)

	China	Moldova	Mongolia	Poland	Russian Federation	Slovak Republic	Ukraine	Vietnam	All
I do not confirm the exchange rate	0.9	6.4	1.8	30.9	7.3	-	-	27.3	9.3
I give the exchange rate information to my relative and he/she confirms it to me	2.7	3.6	0.9	10.0	13.6	-	-	3.6	4.3
My relative asks me about the exchange rate and I confirm whether that was the amount paid	0.9	-	0.9	10.0	1.8	-	-	-	1.7
Other	-	1.8	-	1.8	1.8	-	-	-	0.7
does not know/no response	95.4	88.2	96.4	47.3	75.4	100.0	100.0	69.1	84.0

Written information about the details of the transfer is given to you . . . (Question 7)

	China	Moldova	Mongolia	Poland	Russian Federation	Slovak Republic	Ukraine	Vietnam	All
Before the transaction is completed	56.4	-	60.7	5.5	-	-	-	78.2	25.2
After the transaction is completed	21.8	11.8	24.1	53.6	54.5	-	51.8	10.0	28.5
Before and after the transaction is completed	-	23.6	3.6	1.8	23.6	-	-	10.9	7.9
I do not receive written information	20.9	62.7	7.1	27.3	20.0	15.5	41.8	0.9	24.5
does not know/no response	0.9	1.8	4.5	11.8	1.8	84.5	6.4	-	13.9

Preferred method of sending home money (Question 8)

	China	Moldova	Mongolia	Poland	Russian Federation	Slovak Republic	Ukraine	Vietnam	All
Bank/Credit Union	15.1	10.4	11.0	30.7	6.1	0.6	-	1.1	8.5
Money Transfer Operator	26.0	18.20	41.9	11.4	44.1	-	24.7	46.7	27.7
Post Office with Western Union	4.8	3.6	5.7	8.6	4.5	-	-	0.6	3.3
Post Office with other	-	0.5	0.5	3.6	-	-	0.4	-	0.6
Regular mail	18.5	-	-	2.1	-	-	-	-	2.1
Friends/relatives travelling	35.6	25.0	20.5	28.6	29.6	27.7	39.7	39.4	30.9
Courier	-	31.2	1.0	10.7	9.5	6.5	31.8	-	12.5
ATM	-	7.8	-	-	2.8	-	0.4	-	1.5
Debit/Credit cards	-	1.0	1.9	0.7	-	1.9	-	-	0.7
Mobile phone	-	-	-	-	-	-	-	-	-
Other	-	2.1	17.6	3.6	3.4	63.2	2.9	12.2	12.4

Preferred RSP Type (Question 9)

	China	Moldova	Mongolia	Poland	Russian Federation	Slovak Republic	Ukraine	Vietnam	All
MTO	43	29	85	16	70	-	52	57	44
Friends/Relatives	22	17	1	31	6	13	-	40	16
Bank/Credit Union	13	11	2	18	5	-	-	2	6
Post Office with Other	23	-	-	26	-	-	-	-	6
Post Office with Western Union	-	1	-	-	5	-	-	-	1
Other	-	36	5	6	16	87	48	-	25
does not know/no response	-	6	8	4	-	-	-	1	2

Preferred RSP Name (Question 9)

	China	Moldova	Mongolia	Poland	Russian Federation	Slovak Republic	Ukraine	Vietnam	All
Western Union	39	19	21	15	39	-	10	48	24
Chequepoint	-	6	33	-	32	-	42	-	14
Friends	22	7	1	31	4	10	-	34	14
Bus Driver	-	34	-	5	10	6	43	-	12
Myself	-	2	-	-	4	80	6	-	11
Other MTO	4	6	29	2	3	-	-	9	7
Czech customs post	23	-	-	26	-	-	-	-	6
Other bank	13	11	2	18	5	-	-	2	6
Relatives	-	10	-	-	2	3	-	6	3
Moneygram	-	-	2	-	1	-	-	-	-
Other	-	-	5	1	2	1	-	-	1
does not know/no response	-	6	8	4	-	-	-	1	2

Why do you send money with these methods? (Question 10)

	China	Moldova	Mongolia	Poland	Russian Federation	Slovak Republic	Ukraine	Vietnam	All
It is inexpensive compared to other methods	11.6	24.1	20.3	19.4	18.1	33.2	23.2	11.4	18.9
It is fast	14.6	17.5	18.2	22.5	25.1	13.1	25.6	17.2	18.8
It is safe	17.1	10.9	26.4	19.8	18.1	15.9	15.9	17.9	17.7
It is easy to use/comprehensible	16.6	10.6	13.9	27.7	7.7	27.6	11.6	16.4	16.3
It is conveniently located for the receiver	19.6	26.3	2.0	2.8	23.6	9.2	14.9	17.9	15.1
It is conveniently located for the sender	15.7	9.5	7.1	6.7	6.6	0.7	8.5	19.0	10.6
It does not require an official ID	-	-	-	-	-	-	0.3	-	-
Other	4.8	1.1	12.2	1.2	0.7	0.4	-	0.2	2.5

What source most informs your decision to choose a remittance company? (Question 11)

	China	Moldova	Mongolia	Poland	Russian Federation	Slovak Republic	Ukraine	Vietnam	All
Migrants/friends	27.9	30.4	59.4	40.0	30.3	56.0	35.7	23.0	34.4
Word of mouth	44.1	3.8	23.0	13.3	2.7	16.0	6.8	16.7	13.6
Family at home	2.7	21.2	6.7	9.7	12.2	28.0	21.7	5.0	12.0
TV/radio	19.8	6.5	2.4	1.2	10.9	-	4.8	22.3	10.2
Advertisement in the newspaper	0.9	8.2	1.8	1.2	8.6	-	6.8	21.4	8.7
Internet	0.9	9.8	0.6	12.7	14.0	-	6.4	1.6	6.5
Advertisement on a leaflet in native language	0.9	0.5	4.2	0.6	10.9	-	15.7	2.5	5.6
Advertisement in the streets	1.8	4.9	1.2	0.6	2.7	-	0.0	6.3	2.8
Mass/church	-	-	-	6.1	-	-	0.0	0.3	0.8
Embassy/consulate	-	1.1	-	-	-	-	0.8	-	0.3
Meeting of the migrant association	-	-	-	-	0.5	-	0.4	-	0.1
Other source	0.9	13.6	0.6	14.5	7.2	-	0.8	0.9	5.0

How long are you told at your most used remittance company that it takes for the transfer to be ready for withdrawal? (Question 12)

	China	Moldova	Mongolia	Poland	Russian Federation	Slovak Republic	Ukraine	Vietnam	All
Minutes	39.1	35.5	25.0	10.0	35.5	-	9.1	47.3	25.2
A couple of hours or overnight	-	2.7	11.6	14.5	21.8	14.5	0.9	23.6	11.2
One day	-	32.7	15.2	21.8	24.5	1.8	82.7	15.5	24.3
I am not told how long/is uncertain	-	18.2	-	2.7	4.5	-	-	7.3	4.1
Other	60.9	9.1	44.6	48.2	11.8	-	1.8	6.4	22.9
does not know/no response	-	1.8	1.8	-	1.8	81.8	9.1	2.7	12.3

How do the receivers usually collect the money? (Question 13)

	China	Moldova	Mongolia	Poland	Russian Federation	Slovak Republic	Ukraine	Vietnam	All
Home delivery	22.8	22	3.9	29.1	30.4	90.7	40.9	32.8	34.1
Withdrawal at any outlet of the RSP	43.3	21.2	22.7	15.7	19.6	-	5.5	38.5	20.4
Withdrawal at a specific outlet of the RSP	-	8.5	66.4	7.5	32.3	-	20.5	12.6	18.9
Post office	33.9	1.7	-	9	-	-	-	0.6	4.9
In bank account	-	2.5	-	26.9	2.5	-	-	0.6	3.7
Withdrawal at ATM	-	11	-	0.7	1.9	-	-	0.6	1.5
Mobile phone account	-	-	-	-	-	-	-	-	-
Other	-	33.1	7	11.2	13.3	9.3	33.2	14.4	16.4

When the receivers collect the money . . . (Question 14)

	China	Moldova	Mongolia	Poland	Russian Federation	Slovak Republic	Ukraine	Vietnam	All
Their only choice is to receive in local currency	13.6	6.4	-	48.2	13.6	17.3	-	3.6	12.8
They have a choice to receive in local currency or foreign currency (CZK, USD, EUR, etc)	86.4	90.9	99.1	50.0	82.7	3.6	94.5	96.4	75.5
does not know/no response	-	2.7	0.9	1.8	3.6	79.1	5.5	-	11.7

Have you ever had problems in the past when you have sent the money? (Question 15)

	China	Moldova	Mongolia	Poland	Russian Federation	Slovak Republic	Ukraine	Vietnam	All
Never had a problem	78.6	80.9	83.9	76.8	86.3	92.6	79.3	91.8	83.8
The money arrived with many days of delay	3.6	11.8	12.9	13.4	12.7	1.9	14.1	6.4	9.5
The receiver had to pay a fee to withdraw the money	-	5.5	1.6	0.9	-	-	6.5	-	1.7
The money was not received and you lost everything	3.6	-	-	1.8	-	2.8	-	1.8	1.3
The sum received was not correct	-	0.9	0.8	5.4	1.0	0.9	-	-	1.1
Other	14.3	0.9	0.8	1.8	-	1.9	-	-	2.5

In case of any problem during the sending of your money, which of the following authorities/persons have you contacted/would you contact to request help? (Question 16)

	China	Moldova	Mongolia	Poland	Russian Federation	Slovak Republic	Ukraine	Vietnam	All
The manager of the Money Transfer Operator	-	18.5	41.7	12.6	43.6	4.5	26.2	47.2	27.4
Friends	20.0	16.0	6.8	22.0	23.8	11.4	33.8	39.3	22.2
The director of the Bank/Post Office	80.0	9.2	11.7	37.0	8.1	20.5	1.0	1.1	17.4
The police	-	9.2	15.5	14.2	5.2	59.1	18.5	-	14.9
The management of the agency you send money to	-	1.7	5.8	3.1	12.8	-	12.8	11.8	6.9
The embassy/consulate	-	1.7	9.7	-	0.6	-	-	-	1.9
The general prosecutor	-	-	0.5	-	-	-	-	-	0.1
The financial arbiter	-	-	0.5	-	-	-	-	-	0.1
None of the above	-	22.7	-	6.3	1.7	1.5	0.5	-	3.3
Other	-	21.0	7.8	4.7	4.1	3.0	7.2	0.6	5.9

Would you like to use a more efficient way to send your remittance? (Question 17)

	China	Moldova	Mongolia	Poland	Russian Federation	Slovak Republic	Ukraine	Vietnam	All
I won't change	15.5	72.7	13.4	33.6	45.5	40.0	52.7	49.1	40.2
Direct deposit on a bank account	71.8	18.2	51.8	21.8	29.1	-	3.6	31.8	28.6
Internet	6.4	0.9	10.7	31.8	17.3	24.5	7.3	1.8	12.6
Mobile phone based transfers	1.8	-	9.8	2.7	3.6	16.4	4.5	0.9	5.0
Remittance card	-	0.9	11.6	9.1	-	-	2.7	6.4	3.9
Other	2.7	3.6	2.7	0.9	-	-	-	9.1	2.4
does not know/no response	1.8	3.6	-	-	4.5	19.1	29.1	0.9	7.4

Do you have a bank account? (Question 18)

	China	Moldova	Mongolia	Poland	Russian Federation	Slovak Republic	Ukraine	Vietnam	All
Yes, checking account	52.7	33.6	78.6	72.7	65.5	80.9	49.1	37.3	58.8
Yes, savings account	18.2	-	-	1.8	1.8	-	0.9	6.4	3.6
Yes, both checking and saving	4.5	8.2	-	21.8	12.7	19.1	1.8	28.2	12.0
No	24.5	58.2	21.4	2.7	20.0	-	48.2	27.3	25.3
does not know/no response	-	-	-	0.9	-	-	-	0.9	0.2

Do you have a mobile phone? (Question 19)

	China	Moldova	Mongolia	Poland	Russian Federation	Slovak Republic	Ukraine	Vietnam	*All*
NO	-	-	-	1.8	-	0.9	-	-	*0.3*
YES	100.0	100.0	100.0	97.3	100.0	99.1	100.0	100.0	*99.5*
does not know/no response	-	-	-	0.9	-	-	-	-	*0.1*

What is your sex? (Question 20)

	China	Moldova	Mongolia	Poland	Russian Federation	Slovak Republic	Ukraine	Vietnam	*All*
Female	42	39	61	38	49	19	55	40	*43*
Male	58	61	39	62	51	81	46	60	*57*

Age, length of stay in the Czech Republic, annual income (Question 21, 22, 25)

	China	Moldova	Mongolia	Poland	Russian Federation	Slovak Republic	Ukraine	Vietnam	*All*
Age	34	33	32	36	37	34	37	34	*35*
Length of stay in the Czech Republic	7	5	3	4	6	7	4	7	*5*
Annual income (USD)	12,980	14,995	8,066	20,873	17,731	20,897	14,504	13,560	*15,105*

What type of work do you currently do in the Czech Republic? (Question 23)

	China	Moldova	Mongolia	Poland	Russian Federation	Slovak Republic	Ukraine	Vietnam	All
enterpriser	32.7	11.8	2.7	4.5	29.1	9.1	4.5	48.2	17.8
employee	67.3	72.7	90.2	92.7	60.0	90.9	94.5	40.9	76.2
housewife	-	1.8	1.8	-	0.9	-	0.9	1.8	0.9
student/retired		10.0	3.6	2.7	9.1	-	-	7.3	4.1
unemployed	-	3.6	1.8	-	0.9	-	-	0.9	0.9
other	-	-	-	-	-	-	-	-	-
does not know/no response	-	-	-	-	-	-	-	0.9	0.1

In which sector do you work? (Question 24)

	China	Moldova	Mongolia	Poland	Russian Federation	Slovak Republic	Ukraine	Vietnam	All
agriculture, forestry and fishing	-	17.3	0.9	1.8	-	-	-	-	2.5
manufacturing and other industry	-	15.5	71.4	20.9	3.6	10.0	3.6	5.5	16.4
construction	-	20.9	1.8	17.3	3.6	13.6	23.6	2.7	10.4
wholesale and retail trade	20.0	5.5	4.5	2.7	15.5	7.3	6.4	68.2	16.2
transportation and storage	-	8.2	6.2	5.5	6.4	10.9	3.6	1.8	5.3
accommodation and food service activities	78.2	5.5	8.0	6.4	15.5	5.5	8.2	7.3	16.8
information and communications	1.8	0.9	1.8	6.4	3.6	10.0	10.9	-	4.4
financial and insurance	-	-	-	4.5	7.3	10.0	2.7	-	3.1
real estate activities	-	1.8	-	0.9	10.0	2.7	-	-	1.9
professional, scientific and technical	-	3.6	0.9	9.1	3.6	9.1	0.9	-	3.4
administrative and support services	-	3.6	-	10.9	0.9	7.3	0.9	2.7	3.3
public administration	-	-	-	6.4	-	4.5	-	-	1.4
education	-	1.8	-	0.9	8.2	1.8	3.6	-	2.0
human health and social work activities	-	-	-	2.7	2.7	3.6	13.6	-	2.8
arts entertainment and recreation	-	-	-	-	3.6	-	1.8	-	0.7
other	-	-	-	0.9	4.5	3.6	20.0	2.7	4.0
does not know/no response	-	15.4	4.5	2.7	10.9	-	-	9.1	5.4

What is your legal status in the Czech Republic? (Question 26)

	China	Moldova	Mongolia	Poland	Russian Federation	Slovak Republic	Ukraine	Vietnam	All
Citizen	-	-	-	0.9	3.6	12.7	-	42.7	7.5
Legal resident (living in the Czech Republic for more than 12 months)	99.1	98.2	86.6	90.9	95.5	83.6	100.0	54.5	88.5
Temporary resident (living in the Czech Republic for less than 12 months)	-	1.8	9.8	8.2	0.9	3.6	-	2.7	3.4
Refugee	-	-	-	-	-	-	-	-	-
Illegal resident	0.9	-	3.6	-	-	-	-	-	0.6
does not know/no response	-	-	-	-	-	-	-	-	-

List of Locations

Airport—Prague Ruzyne
Andel
Andel bus station
Andel market
Andel Shopping centre
Arbat (Russian stores chain)
Belehorska
Budejovicka
Call shop at Muzeum
Car repair center in Prague 6
Cerny most
Cerny most—Car factory
Cerny most—Dormitory
Chinese-language school
CIM
Consulate of Ukraine
Consulate of Vietnam
CULS
Dejvicka Prague 6
Embassy of Moldova
Embassy of Mongolia
Embassy of Poland
Embassy of the Slovak Rep.
Flora
Flora shopping centre
Florenc bus station/market
Florenc market
Foreign Police Dpt. Florenc

Foreign Police Dpt. Pankrac
Foreign Police Dpt. Sdruzeni
Haje
Havlickuv Brod
HKH market
Holesovice area
Holesovice market
Hospital Na Homolce
Hospital Na Homolke
Hostel in Prague 10
Hradcany in Prague 6
Hradec Kralove
Huawei Technologies
Jiriho z podebrad
Kacerov metro station
Kalinka (Russian store) Prague 5
Kalinka (Russian store) Prague 6
Kladno
Kladno hostel
Kobylisy
Kolbenova market
Kolbenova metro station
Letenske Namesti
Libus
Main train station
Metropole Shopping centre
Metrostav Construction Site Prague 7
Namesti Miru

Opatov
Opletalova
Opletalova
Palac Akropolis
Pankrac market
Pardubice
Plzen—Car factory
Plzen Central bus station
Plzen Panasonic
Polish church
Polish Institute of Prague
Russian bookstore
SAPA Market
Shestka Shopping centre
Skalka
Slavia Praha stadium
Slovak Church in Prague 1
Staromestska
Strachov football court
Strasnicka market
U Kocura Pub
University Hospital Motol
Ustek
Vrsovicka
Vysocanska
Wenceslas Square
Zelivskeho bus station
Zlute lazne Prague 4

A CNB Study on "Remittances from the Czech Republic"

This section contains a study on remittances in Czech Republic elaborated by Petr Sedlacek of the Czech National Bank. The study does not necessarily reflect the opinions of the World Bank Group. Moreover, it should be noted that the methodology used to calculate remittance flows is not the same as the methodology used by the World Bank, and data on remittance flows published by the World Bank might not be comparable with data presented here.

Introduction

In recent decades, remittances from the Czech Republic have become an important source of income for many developing countries, a fact that has prompted the Czech authorities to start paying attention to this issue.

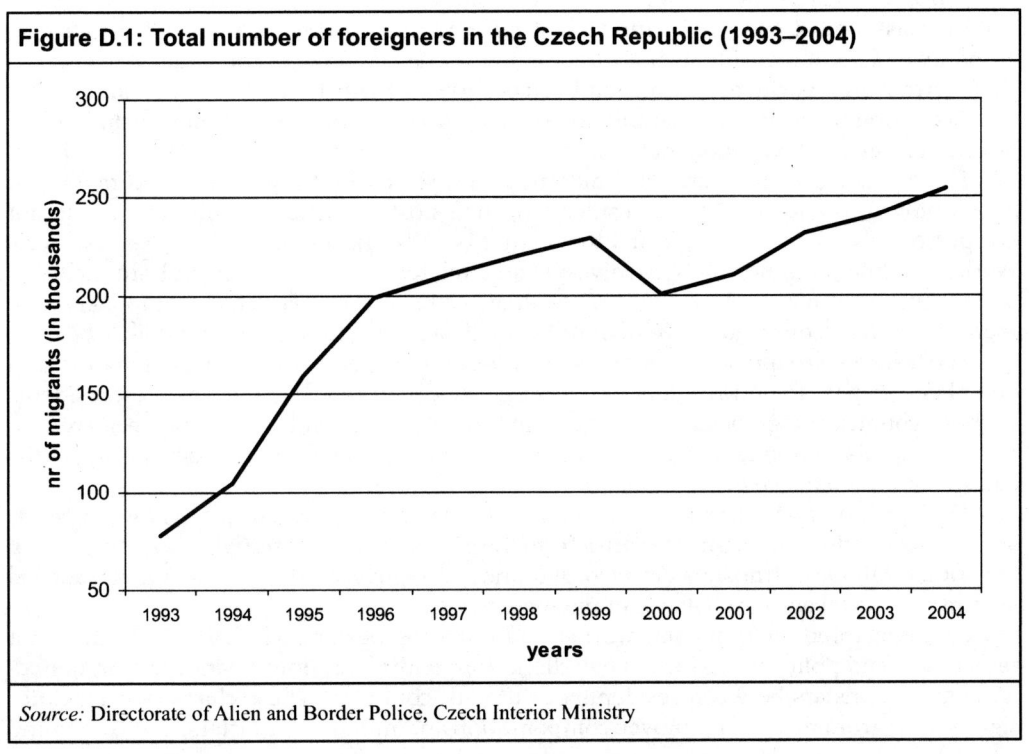

Figure D.1: Total number of foreigners in the Czech Republic (1993–2004)

Source: Directorate of Alien and Border Police, Czech Interior Ministry

Remittances from the Czech Republic have existed since 1993. The Czech Republic has moved from being a traditional source of emigrants to an immigration destination. With the exception of 2000, the number of migrants has risen steadily since 1993.[1]

In the early 1990s there was no methodology for measuring this type of financial flow. Therefore, the Czech Statistical Office (CSO), in cooperation with the Czech National Bank (CNB), started collecting data on income, old-age pensions, taxes, and other allowances as an equivalent of remittances. These elements were entered as a part of other current transfers under the private international transfers sub-item.

Since 2005, the CSO and the CNB have updated the methodology for estimating migration and remittance flows, using as a basis the fifth edition of the Balance of Payments Manual (BPM5) (IMF 1993). The new approach differs considerably from the previous one, and comparison between data produced is not possible. Therefore, this paper focuses only on data available as of 2005.

This "pilot paper" aims to provide basic information on remittance flows out of the Czech Republic since 2005 and, if possible, to determine domestic factors affecting these flows. Macroeconomic conditions in the Czech Republic and demographic characteristics of migrants are important determinants of remittances.

Target countries were selected on based on their importance as the source of migrants. The seven most important countries are treated individually. Two members of the European Union (EU)—the Slovak Republic and Poland—were included because of their importance as neighboring emigration countries. At the aggregate level, the data was consolidated into three groups.[2]

Definitions and Measurements

Remittances are essentially funds that an economy derives from its citizens and their relatives working abroad. These include funds that flow through formal channels, such as electronic transfers, or through informal channels, such as cash carried across borders. They consist almost entirely of funds sent by individuals who have migrated to a new economy and became residents there and of net compensation of border, seasonal, or other short-term workers who are employed in an economy of which they are not residents.[3]

According to the BPM5, compilation of statistics on remittances should include three balance-of-payments components.

The first component, workers' remittances, records current transfers by migrants who are employed in and considered residents of their host countries. In this case, a migrant is a person who stays or is expected to stay in his or her host country for a year or more. Workers' remittances normally involve persons related to one another and are recorded under current transfers. The workers' remittances balance-of-payments component best represents what economists have in mind when developing remittances models.

The second component, employee compensation, comprises wages, salaries, and other benefits paid to non-resident workers for work performed for, and paid by, residents of those countries (e.g., border and seasonal workers; local embassy employees are also included in this component). Compensation of employees is recorded under income in the current account balance of payments.

The third component, migrants' transfers, is defined as contra-entries to flows of goods and changes in financial items that arise from the migration of individuals from one country to another. Migrants' transfers are recorded under nongovernment-sector capital transfers item in the capital account balance of payments.

Of these three components, workers' remittances best matches the definition that researchers and policymakers use when discussing remittance flows: periodic, unrequited, nonmarket transfers between residents of different countries. These characteristics differ significantly from those of employee compensation and migrants' transfers, and combining these three items into a single measure of remittances, as is common practice, can often lead to erroneous conclusions.

There is no clear economic justification for treating migrants' transfers and employee compensation as equivalent to workers' remittances. The flows assigned to these three categories reflect different economic effects, or, in the case of migrants' transfers and employee compensation, may be illustrating something other than actual transfers.

Remittance outflows in the Czech statistics include workers' remittances and employee compensations. The quarterly data are based on the statistics of the CSO.

Summary of Facts and Trends

The total amount of annual remittances in nominal terms during the period 2005 to 2009 ranged from CZK 44 billion to CZK 56 billion, as shown in table D.1.

It is more interesting to analyze the flows of remitted amounts by major recipient countries and aggregated groupings (see table D.2 below and table D.12—quarterly remittances—in the annex).

Figures D.2 to D.4 show the raw remittance data grouped by volume. For all countries, except Poland and the Slovak Republic, remittances show an upward trend with a slowdown in the last two quarters (see table D.11 in the annex). This slowdown corresponds closely to the drop (in absolute terms) in Czech Real Gross Domestic Product (RGDP) that occurred in the third quarter of 2008. Poland, where remittances dropped in late 2007, seems to have peaked earlier than the other countries, while the trend in remittances to the Slovak Republic is still declining. The fact that remittances do not follow the same pattern for all

Table D.1: Total remittances in nominal terms in the Czech Republic 2005–2009 (CZK millions)

2005	2006	2007	2008	2009 (IQ+ IIQ)
43,668	35,781	45,003	55,577	29,079

Source: CSO and CNB database and author's calculations.

Table D.2: Annual remittances in nominal terms (CZK millions)

	2005	2006	2007	2008	2009 (IQ+IIQ)	Total
China[4]	210	280	579	680	386	2,135
Poland	487	1 254	1 710	799	642	4,892
Republic of Moldova	557	884	1 237	3 004	1,091	6,773
Russian Federation	1,804	1,679	1,978	2,525	1,476	9,462
Slovak Republic	15,204	7738	7,465	4,489	3,529	42,890
Ukraine	11,698	12,263	17,103	21,999	11,030	74,090
Vietnam	2,168	1,489	2,641	5,468	2,653	14,419
Other EMEs and LICs	2,949	3,717	5,486	6846	3,706	22,704
Total	35,377	29,304	38,199	45,810	24,513	173,203
All countries	43,668	35,781	45,003	55,577	29,079	209,108

Source: CSO and CNB database and author's calculations.

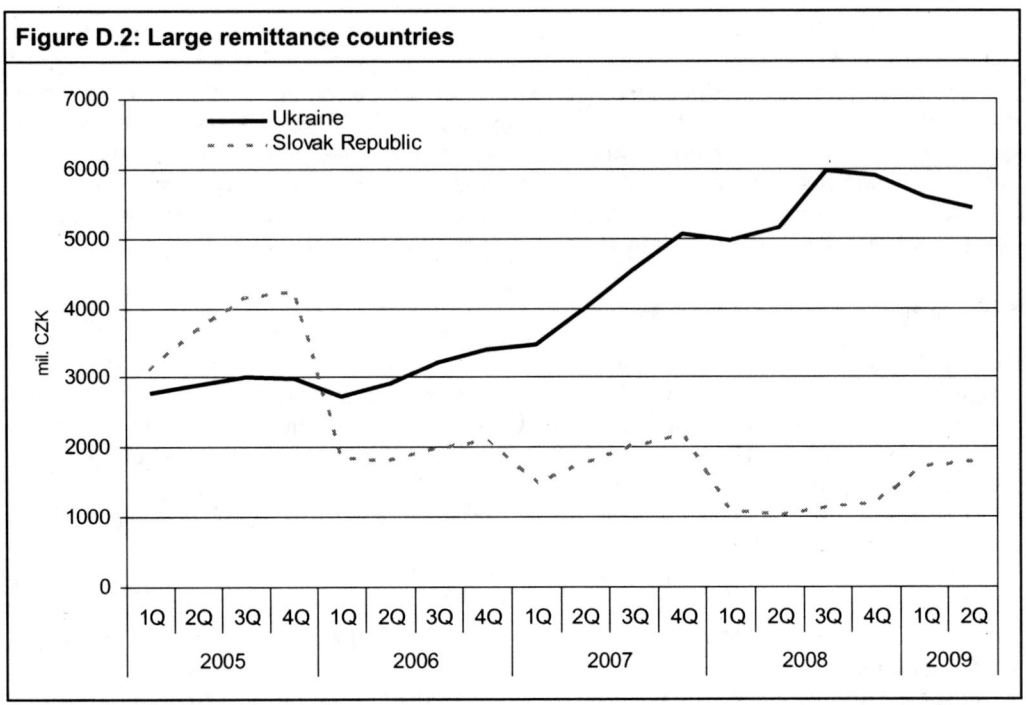

Figure D.2: Large remittance countries

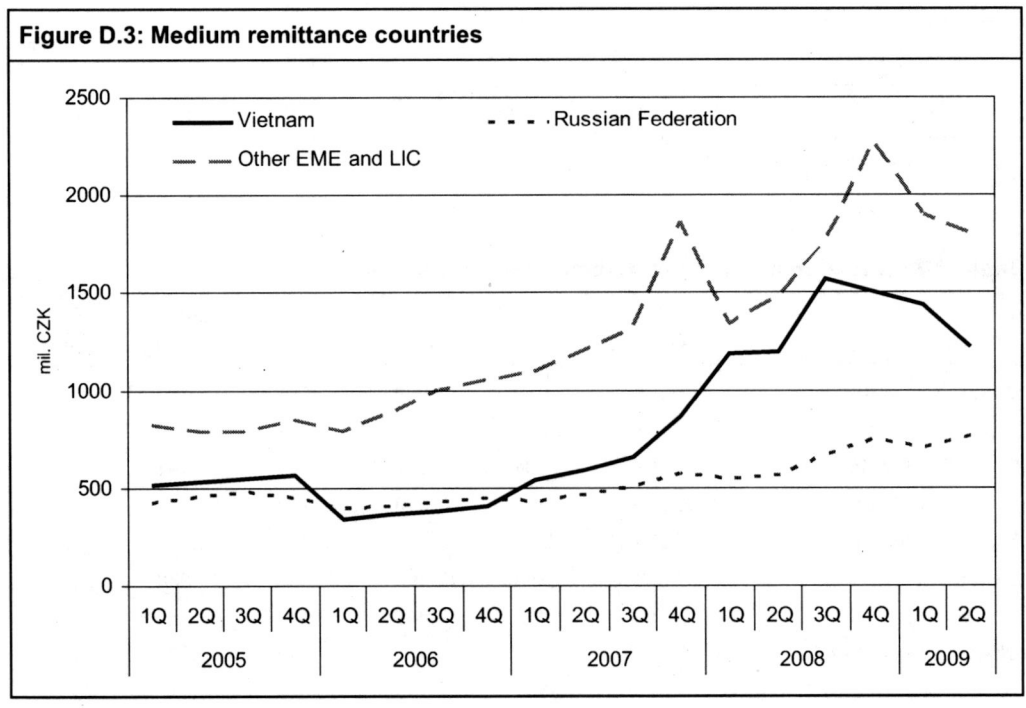

Figure D.3: Medium remittance countries

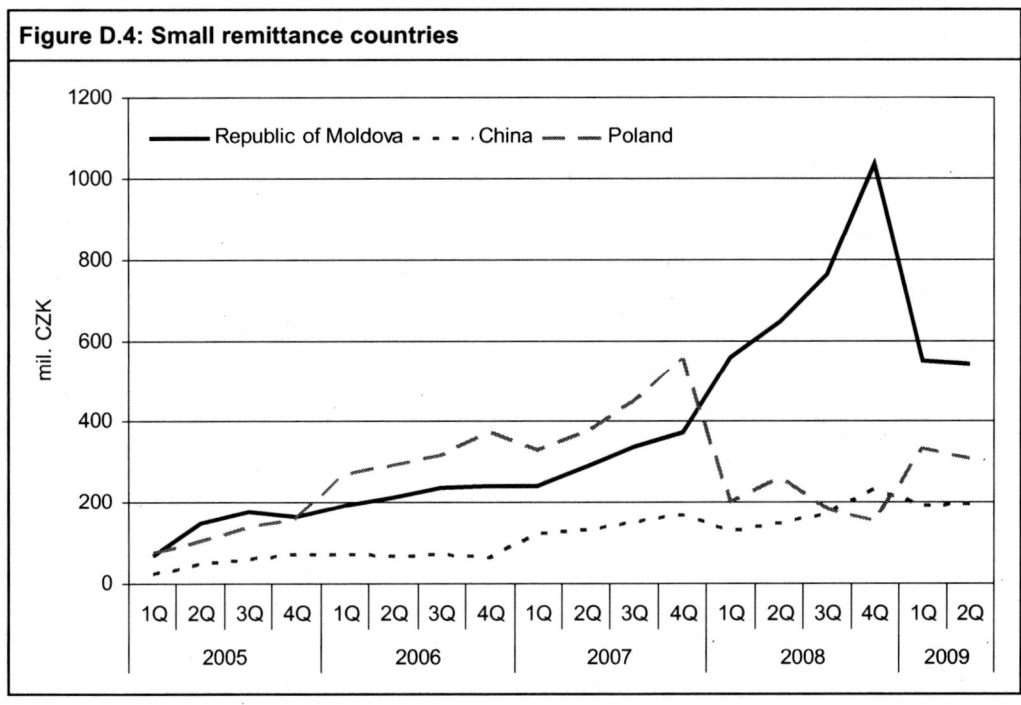

Figure D.4: Small remittance countries

countries suggests that, at a disaggregated level, the economic situation in the host country is not always a determining factor.

The most important country is Ukraine, whose share exceeds 42 percent of total remittances, followed by the Slovak Republic, Vietnam, the Russian Federation, the Republic of Moldova, Poland, and China. The declining trend in remittances to the Slovak Republic and Poland is dwarfed by that of the other countries, even though the proportion of remittances going to these two countries is relatively high. Initially, Poland and the Slovak Republic accounted for about 40 percent of total remittances, but as their absolute value decreased and that of all the other countries grew, the proportion fell to 17 percent. Such a large change in the distribution by country of total remittances is quite interesting, considering the very short time series under consideration.

At the aggregate level, the countries in the "Total" group account for the majority of remittances, with an 82 to 85 percent share of the total amount. Figure D.5 shows the aggregated remittances.[5] The share of developed countries is between 15.1 and 18.1 percent. These flows consist predominantly of wages and remuneration of top managers and experts working temporarily in the Czech Republic.

Table D.3 illustrates the size of remittances in terms of nominal Gross Domestic Product (GDP).

Remittances to "All countries," in terms of nominal GDP, range between 1.12 and 1.53 percent. Despite the financial and economic crisis, remittances in terms of GDP have increased during 2008 with two exceptions—those to the Slovak Republic and Poland. One possible explanation could be the behavior of migrants, who tried to maintain the level of support to their relatives hit by the crisis in their home country. The fact that nature of the business cycle in the Slovak Republic and Poland seems to influence remittances tends to indicate once again that the business cycle in home countries is more important than that in the Czech Republic.

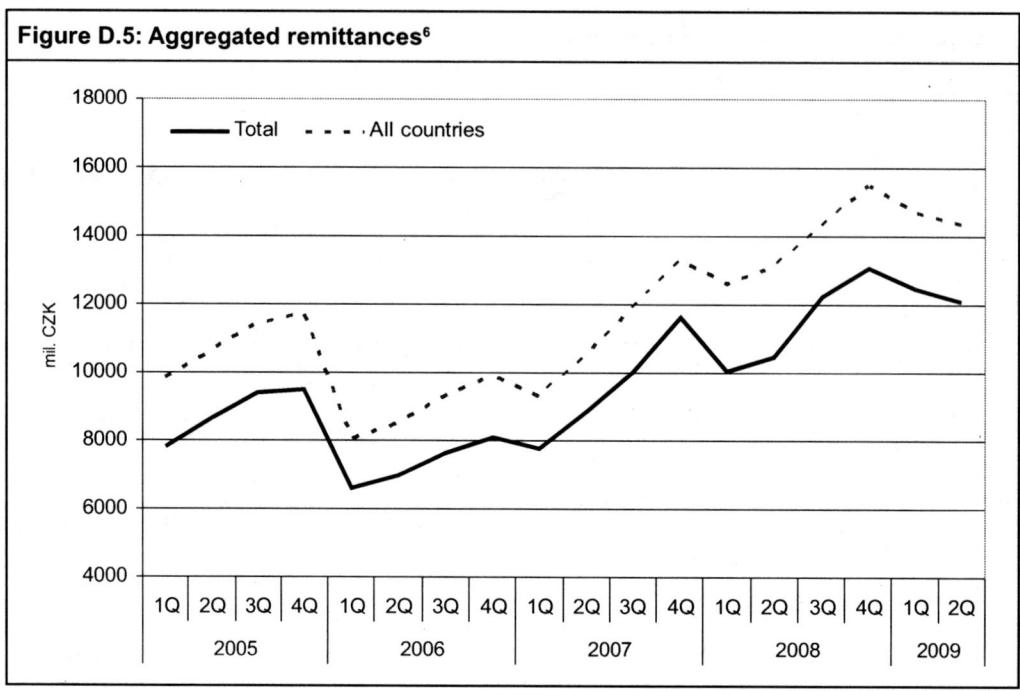

Figure D.5: Aggregated remittances[6]

Table D.4 illustrates the growth rates of remittances.

Growth in nominal terms of remittances under "Total" slightly decelerated in 2008, going from 21.4 percent (2007) to 13.3 percent (2008). Despite this deceleration, the growth rate remained comparable to the 2008 world growth rate of remittances to developing countries (+15%).[7]

Clear differences exist between regions.[8] The growth rate of remittances to the Commonwealth of Independent States (CIS) and the Russian Federation is dynamic, while the growth rate of remittances to Central Europe (Poland and the Slovak Republic) is decelerating. In countries of developing Asia, there was steady remittance rate growth

Table D.3: Remittances in terms of nominal GDP—annual averages (in %)

	2005	2006	2007	2008
China	0.01	0.01	0.02	0.02
Poland	0.02	0.04	0.05	0.02
Republic of Moldova	0.02	0.03	0.03	0.08
Russian Federation	0.06	0.05	0.06	0.07
Slovak Republic	0.51	0.24	0.21	0.12
Ukraine	0.39	0.38	0.48	0.60
Vietnam	0.07	0.05	0.07	0.15
Other EMEs and LICs	0.11	0.12	0.15	0.19
Total	1.19	0.91	1.08	1.24
All countries	1.46	1.11	1.27	1.50

Source: CSO and CNB database and author's calculations.

Table D.4: Annual growth rates of remittances (in %)

	2006	2007	2008
China	25.9	92.3	10.9
Poland	142.1	27.1	−55.9
Republic of Moldova	45.3	30.4	129.4
Russian Federation	−12.8	9.7	20.5
Slovak Republic	−52.2	−10.2	−43.2
Ukraine	−1.8	29.9	21.5
Vietnam	−35.6	65.1	95.6
Other EMEs and LICs	7.1	37.5	18
Total	−22.3	21.4	13.3
All countries	−23.2	17.2	16.2

Source: CSO and CNB database and author's calculations.

to Vietnam, but for China the rate fell in 2008 from its remarkable 2007 peak (the highest growth rate among all countries).

Nominal per capita remittances in Czech Crowns show no general trends (see table D.5).

The average quarterly remitted per capita amount is highest for the CIS and the Russian Federation, a fact that can be explained by the very strong altruistic support of relatives in the home countries. In developing Asia, there are disparities between the levels of remittances to China, where the average quarterly per capita remittance ranged from CZK 29,488 to CZK 36,727, and Vietnam, where the range was between CZK 9,550 and CZK 24,107. The lower level of remittances to Vietnam could be explained by the fact that families from Vietnam are more integrated in the Czech Republic and therefore have already weaker ties to their home country than migrants from China. In Central Europe, remittances to the Slovak Republic have declined rapidly, and those to Poland have fluctuated widely. The time series

Table D.5: Quarterly per capita remittances (annual averages in Czech koruna)

	2005	2006	2007	2008
China	32,970.6	29,487.5	33,034.4	36,726.9
Poland	8,154.8	17,956.5	17,340.0	9,203.2
Republic of Moldova	31,236.2	30,067.4	42,154	41,442.6
Russian Federation	27,844.0	23,116.2	23,029.1	24,884.4,
Slovak Republic	40,536.4	17,027.7	14,630.7	8,006.3
Ukraine	34,886.0	32,039.6	36,512.8	42,166.2
Vietnam	15,085.6	9,545.8	14,272.8	24,107.1
Other EMEs and LICs	25,312	23,872.9	27,417.9	29,449.4
Total	31,301.7	22,026.7	23,935.9	25,120.9
All countries	34,422.9	24,236.3	25,478.2	28,144.5

Source: CSO and CNB database and author's calculations.

is too short to provide an economic explanation for these differences. Explanations should rather be sought in the methodology of remittance calculations. The narrowing economic gap between the Czech Republic and the Slovak Republic could explain the declining trend of remittances to the Slovak Republic.

Remittance Determinants

What are the factors in the Czech Republic that affect the remittances flows?

The relationship between the remitter and his or her family can generally be characterized in two ways: as altruism, in which remittances may compensate for poor economic performance at home, or as a self-interested exchange, in which the family derives no pecuniary services from the remitter. Either motivation, as well as the unique relationship among family members, implies that the characteristics of remittance flows differ from those of profit-driven private capital flows.

Existing literature on the causes of remittances lists the main variables that drive remittances and can help predict a potential relationship between these causal factors and the size and timing of remittance flows. Surprisingly, little has been written on the impact on remittance flows of the host country's economic conditions.

Remittance flows from the Czech Republic should respond to changes in the country's macroeconomic conditions and in the demographic features of migrants residing there.

The following variables were tested to verify if they affected remittances:

A. Economic Conditions in the Czech Republic

Real GDP

Existing literature has widely reported on the correlation between real GDP and workers' remittances series. An improvement in the host country's economic conditions would most likely be accompanied by an improvement in the economic conditions of migrants, if household consumption is considered a normal good. Generally, increases in the host country's economic conditions are associated with increases in remittance flows.

At the aggregate level, there are a number of compelling theoretical and empirical reasons to suspect that there is no long-term relationship between aggregate remittance flows to a particular country and the level of GDP (or other income or activity measurements) in the host country. A number of other factors, some of which are unobservable, could cause structural shocks to this relationship, including home country income, earnings potential, the socio-demographic profile of migrants, stock of migrants, and average length of stay. The short sample periods also present a challenge to proving this hypothesis.

Unemployment

Because it can result in the possible social marginalization of migrants, the unemployment rate is a better gauge of migrants' income than the GDP. Fluctuations in the unemployment rate would have repercussions on the number of employed migrants and therefore on the level of remittance flows. In this case, a decrease in unemployment should be accompanied by an improvement in migrants' economic conditions and result in increased remittances.

Income

A migrant's income is an important variable insofar as it defines the economic situation for his/her family. Observations are based on the average nominal wage in the Czech Republic, to compensate for the fact that migrants' remuneration varies according to the different types of economic activity in which they engage. Changes in remittance outflows should normally reflect a rise in the average nominal wage.

Variables Related to Monetary Policy

Monetary policy–related variables can indicate expected future changes in the Czech economic conditions. These variables include the reference rate (2W Repo rate), which, according to Bernanke and Blinder (1992), is the best available measure of monetary policy. An increase in the 2W Repo rate (contractionary monetary policy) can have a negative effect on the Czech Republic's economic conditions, which in turn would lead to a decrease in remittances, and vice versa.

The M2 as a measure of monetary policy is also considered as a determinant. This variable reflects past monetary policy. A positive shock to M2 (expansionary monetary policy) can be related to higher income and lower interest rates in the Czech Republic, with positive effects on remittances.

Exchange Rate Differentials (Euro, U.S. dollar)

The exchange rate is defined as Czech koruna per Euro or United States dollar, the main currencies used by migrants in remitted transfers. Changes in exchange rates in sending or receiving countries may influence the volume of remittance flows. Depreciation of the host country's currency may reduce remittances to home countries, as most families in the Czech Republic base their contributions on their level of income and on predetermined amounts in Czech koruna, and send them in Euros or U.S. dollars.

B. Demographic Features

Demographic characteristics are thought to be associated with remittances, and there is general agreement on the effect of many of these variables on the amounts remitted. These characteristics include the size of the stock of migrants, length of stay, average income level, and gender.

The stock of migrants (see table D.11 in the annex) is a natural determinant of remittances. Calculations are based on CSO data, as they are more comprehensive than police statistics. The total number of migrants is divided into two categories: residents and non-residents. Residents are migrants staying the Czech Republic for one year or more, non-residents are migrants staying less than one year. The total number of foreigners includes estimated data on illegal migrants. A rise in the stock of migrants should logically result in a corresponding rise in remittances flows.

Quantifying immigration is always problematic, as illegal immigration figures are necessarily incomplete and often conflicting. Official and informal estimates vary widely.

Gender affects the level of income of the migrants and short-term workers, because women often have lower average incomes than men. Relevant gender disaggregated data is available for only three years of the latest five-year series, and is thus unusable for the purposes of present study.

Migrants' duration of stay is also a determining variable, because the longer a migrant stays in the host country, the more his/her motivation to remit declines. This may be due to the relaxation of ties with the home country. In most instances, short-term workers consume less of their income than migrants, and therefore more of their income or compensation is available to support family members in their home country. Short-term workers maintain strong ties with their country of origin because of their permanent interest in their home

Table D.6: Trend in illegal migration of foreigners in the Czech Republic (2000–2007)

2000	2001	2002	2003	2004	2005	2006	2007
53 116	39 399	32 2005	32 475	26 129	14 545	10 793	7 549

Source: Czech Police Headquarters.

countries. Results should be assessed with caution, as migrants' capacity to remit often increases also because their income tends to rise over time.

C. What Drives Remittance Flows—Empirical Investigations

The time series for this study is extremely short, making any analysis highly descriptive. There is little room for understanding simple correlations of variables and no room for formal econometric analysis. This is especially troublesome since relations between variables can only be described separately, without the possibility of checking for other effects. Thus, all conclusions are only partial explanations and only indicative, since it is not possible to differentiate the effects of individual explanatory variables.

The Czech Republic encounters statistical problems that are similar to those of other countries. Data on remittance flows are not systematically reported, and a geographical breakdown of remittance flows to third countries is available only for some countries. In most countries there is a minimum threshold for remittances, below which individual transfers are simply not recorded. While some countries estimate the transfers below this threshold in the balance of payments, many others simply ignore them and thus underestimate remittances. Analyzing the evolution of remittances over time is also problematic, as improvements in reporting systems, lower transaction costs, and a potential shift from informal to formal channels of remittance flows all complicate the intertemporal comparability of data.

Number of Migrants

It is not surprising that the relation between remittances to a certain country and the number of migrants from that country residing in the Czech Republic is very close. This is demonstrated when comparing the proportion of remittances to a certain country with the proportion of migrants from that same country living in the host country. Interestingly, although Ukrainian migrants account for about 30 percent of total migrants (on average), remittances flowing to Ukraine account for more than 40 percent of total remittances. On

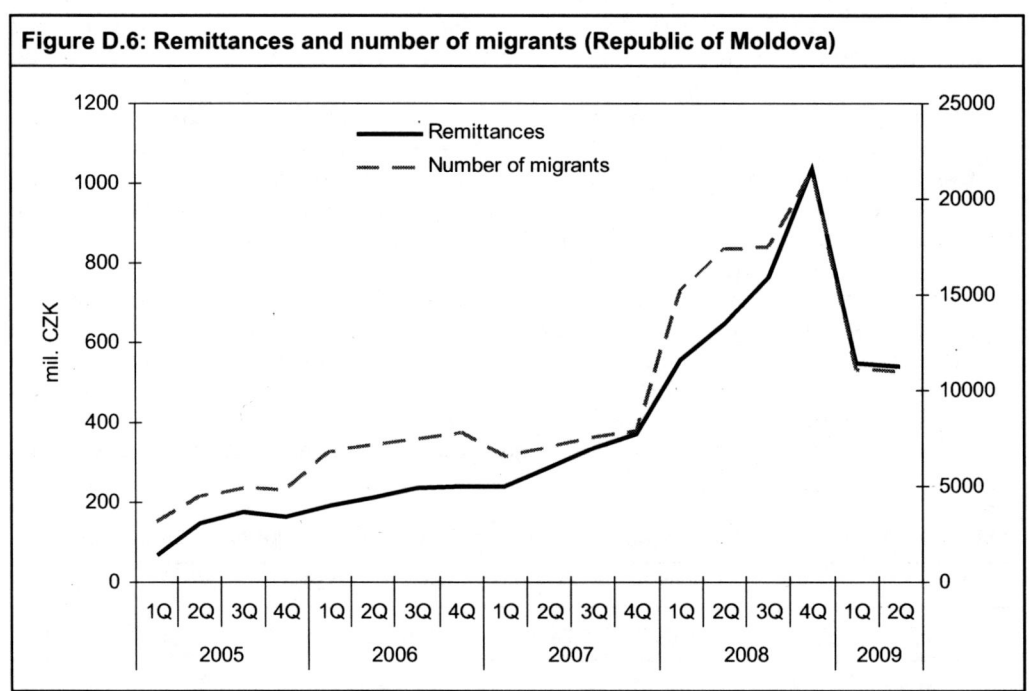

Figure D.6: Remittances and number of migrants (Republic of Moldova)

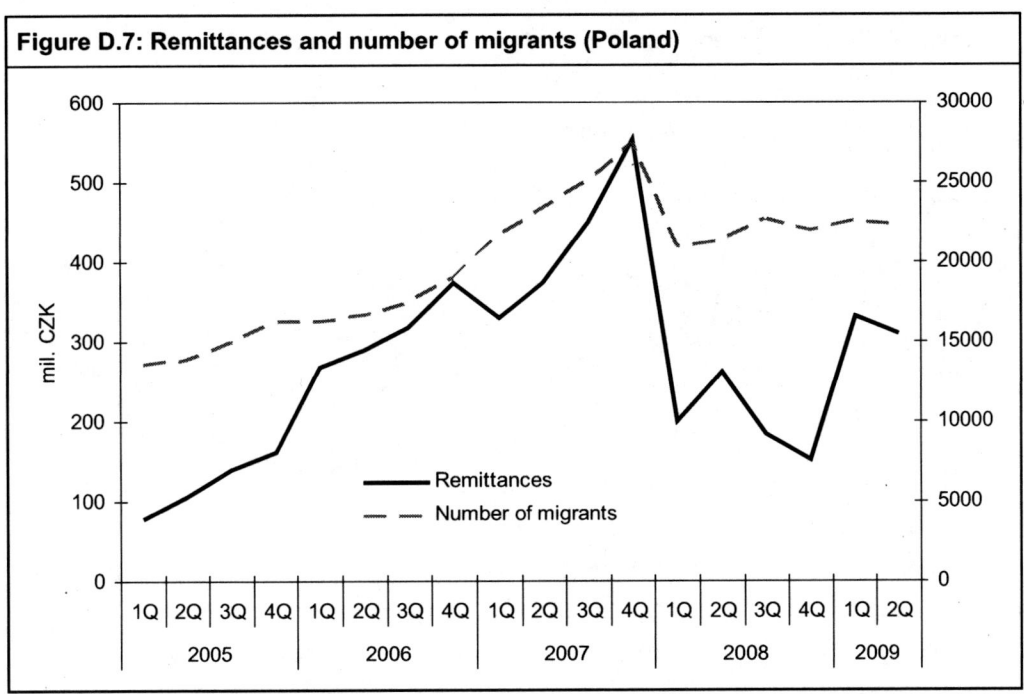

Figure D.7: Remittances and number of migrants (Poland)

the other hand, Vietnam, Poland, and the Slovak Republic have the opposite tendency: the flow of remittances to these countries as a fraction of the total is lower than the same fraction for the number of migrants.[9] This could give a rough indication about the nature of jobs undertaken by the migrants.

Overall, an increase in the number of migrants explains the trend of remittance flows very well. Just to highlight a few countries, figures D.6 to D.8 show some of these developments. Figure D.6 (Republic of Moldova) shows a very close relationship between the number of migrants and the flow of remittances.

The sharp drop in remittances in the last two quarters is fully explained by a similar fall in the number of migrants. On the other hand, Polish flows of remittances are much more sensitive to changes in the number of migrants (figure D.7).

Finally, the only exception from the entire group is the Slovak Republic (figure D.8).

The number of migrants from the Slovak Republic has increased steadily, whereas the remittance flows fell overall. For all countries combined, the overall growth in remittance flows corresponds closely to the increase in the number of migrants (figure D.9).

Interestingly, the very small sample shows that there is a very close correlation between the cyclical variations in the number of migrants and the GDP cycle in the Czech Republic (correlations range from 0.66 for Ukraine to 0.92 for Vietnam). One major exception is the Slovak Republic, where the correlation is negative (–0.39), which drags down the correlation for all countries combined to 0.29. This exception hints at the possibility that Slovak migrants had a different "purpose" when coming to the Czech Republic. It seems that working in the Czech Republic is a way to survive difficult periods in the Slovak Republic (as will be pointed out later, the cycles of both countries are closely correlated). In good times, Slovaks prefer to return home, which might have something to with the countries' proximity. The opposite is true for migrants from the other countries, for whom the Czech Republic seems to be a place where to work only in periods of prosperity.

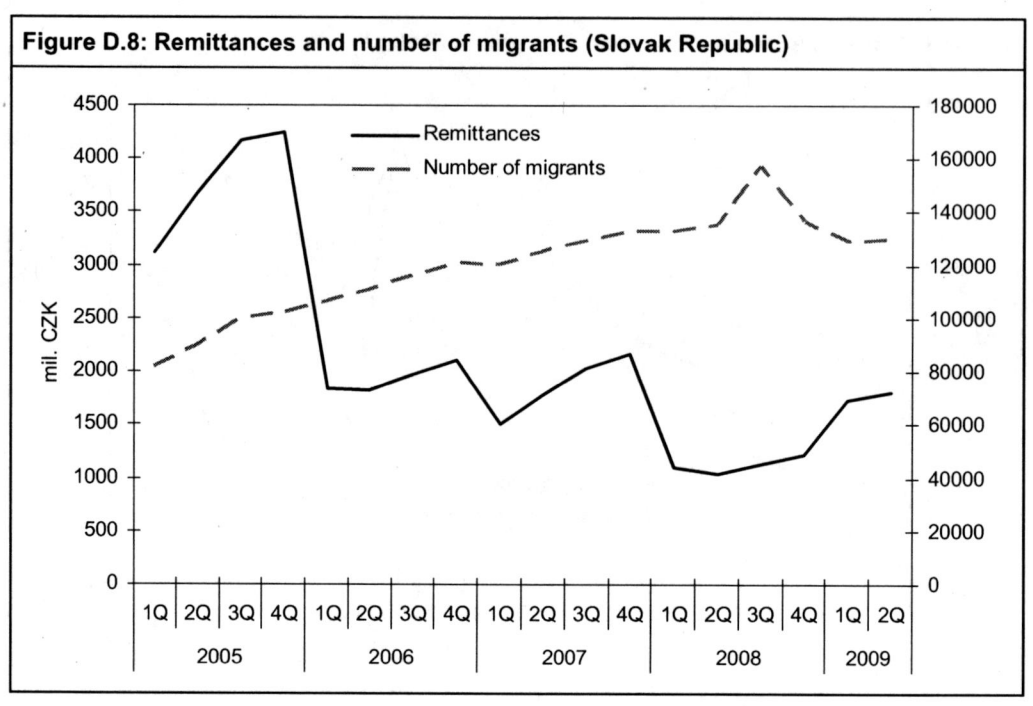

Figure D.8: Remittances and number of migrants (Slovak Republic)

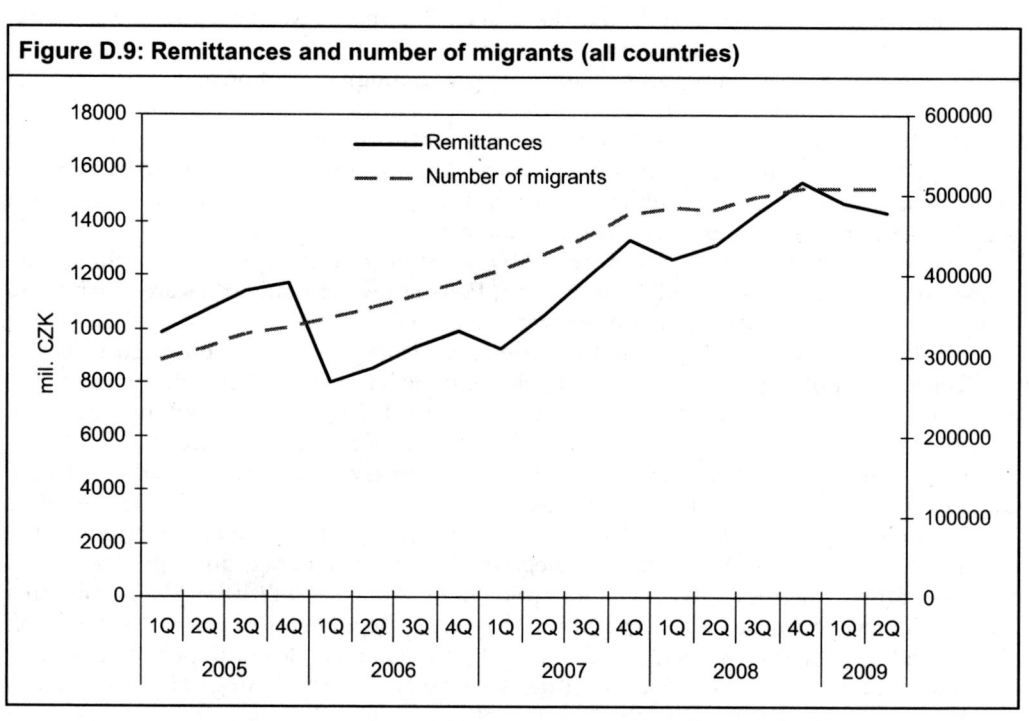

Figure D.9: Remittances and number of migrants (all countries)

Table D.7: Correlations of remittances with the Czech GDP cycle

	H-P Filtered	YoY Growth Rates
Ukraine	0.35	0.15
Vietnam	0.12	−0.01
Russian Federation	−0.38	−0.73
Republic of Moldova	0.47	0.19
China	0.24	0.25
Poland	0.03	0.41
Slovak Republic	−0.58	−0.75
Other EMEs and LICs	0.07	−0.06
Total	**−0.10**	**−0.34**
All countries	**−0.07**	**−0.30**

Source: CSO and author's calculations.

Host and Native Country GDP Cycles

One of the explanatory variables used in pertinent literature is the host country's (in this case, the Czech Republic) economic cycle. When looking at the real GDP series, it is difficult to grasp the relationship between the GDP cycle and remittances. The reason is that the end of the time series is characterized by a sharp decline, and filtering methods (especially the commonly used H-P filter) are known for their end-point problem.[10] For this reason, the study focuses not only on the cycle described by the H-P filter, but also on year-to-year growth rates. Figure D.10 (see the annex) displays the two series, showing the large discrepancy. Any statements about co-movement of remittances with the cycle must thus be very cautious.

The correlations between remittances and the GDP cycle are summarized in table D.7.

Total remittances turn out to be weakly countercyclical with the Czech business cycle. Thus, in difficult periods, remittances increase, and in prosperous periods foreign workers send smaller remittances. It is noteworthy, however, that the aggregate figures hide interesting inter-country differences. The negative correlation is driven mainly by the Russian Federation and the Slovak Republic, both of which are strongly counter-cyclical while at the same time accounting for approximately a third of all remittances. On the other hand, Ukraine (the country with the largest volume of remittances) is weakly pro-cyclical,

Table D.8: Correlation of remittances with native GDP cycle

	H-P Filtered	YoY Growth Rates
China		0.44
Poland	0.11	−0.01
Russian Federation	−0.30	−0.35
Slovak Republic	−0.43	−0.61
Ukraine	0.19	0.24

Source: Datastream and author's calculations.

as are the Republic of Moldova and China. Vietnam and the group of other EME and LIC countries are not characterized by any clear cyclicality.

For comparative purposes, the GDP cycle in five native countries was used to explain remittance behavior. Table D.8 summarizes the correlation of remittances with the economic situation in the native country.

Once again, there is no clear picture for all the countries. The Russian Federation and the Slovak Republic are counter-cyclical, whereas Ukraine and China are pro-cyclical. Remittances to Poland seem to be independent of the business cycle.

The concomitant movement of remittances and the business cycle in the host and native countries seems to be the same. This is not surprising once one looks at the correlations of the business cycles across countries. All correlations are highly positive, above 0.7.

Unemployment

For reasons stated in the main text, unemployment in the host country could be an explanatory variable for remittances. Unemployment in the Czech Republic has fallen steadily during the previous four years, only to start slowly moving upwards in mid 2008 (figure D.10).

Hence, the steady increase and subsequent decline in remittances in the last two quarters common to most of the countries can be related to the evolution of unemployment rates. Similarly, the correlations of the cyclical component of unemployment are negatively related to the cyclical components of remittance flows (–0.29 for all countries). This average masks a high level of heterogeneity (as was the case for the GDP). The Slovak Republic and the Russian Federation have a positive correlation between the unemployment rate and remittance flows at business cycle frequencies (0.27 and 0.42, respectively). On the other hand, Ukraine, Vietnam, the Republic of Moldova, and China have negative correlations (–0.52, –0.15, –0.48, and –0.32, respectively). However, as it is clear that the unemployment rate is closely related to the business cycle, it is doubtful that in this narrow sample the unemployment rate can provide information beyond that of the GDP fluctuations analyzed earlier.

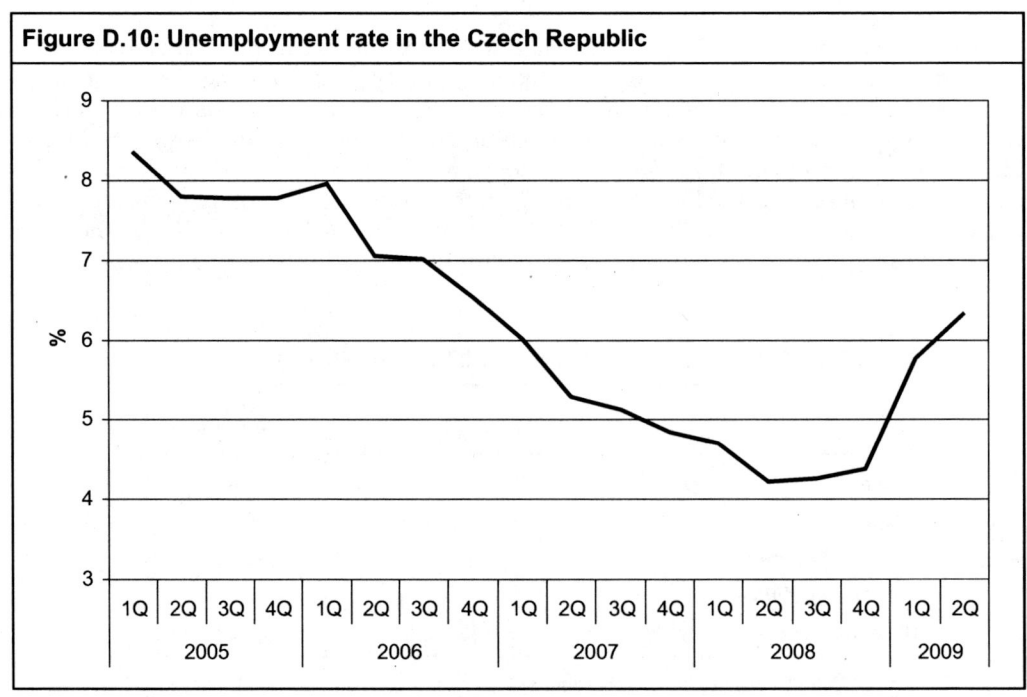

Figure D.10: Unemployment rate in the Czech Republic

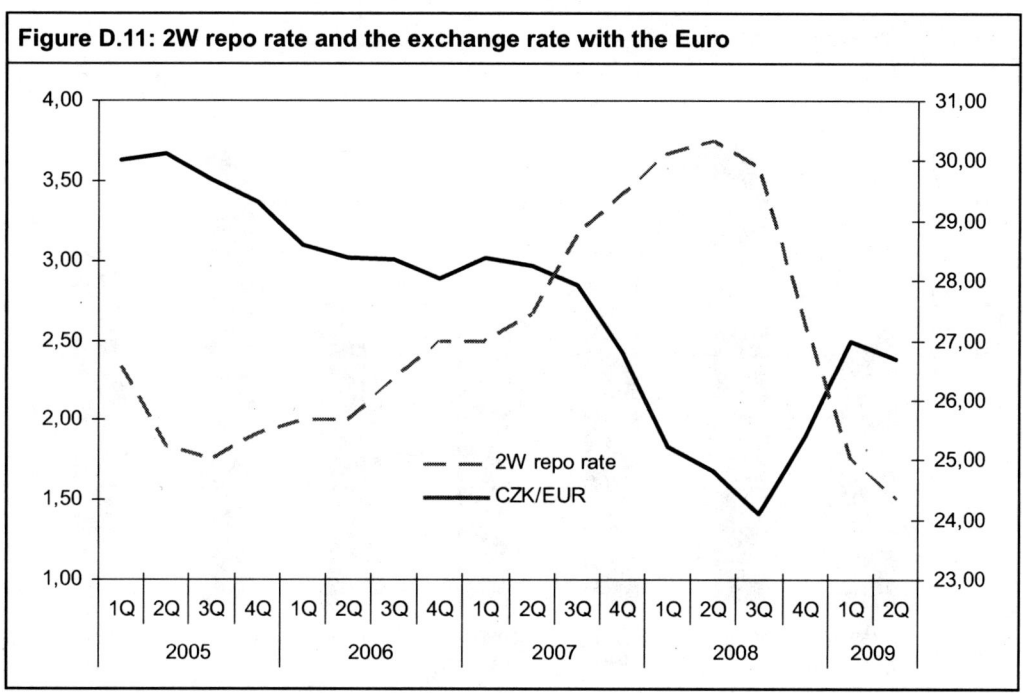

Figure D.11: 2W repo rate and the exchange rate with the Euro

Legend:
- 2W repo rate
- CZK/EUR

The Interest and Exchange Rate

Figure D.11 shows the 2W repo rate and the exchange rate with the Euro.

Figure D.11 shows how closely linked monetary policy in the Czech Republic is to the exchange rate. Both variables indicate that remittances were probably rising until the end of 2007; a subsequent sharp increase in the repo rate and a corresponding decrease in the exchange rate should lead, all things being equal, to a decrease in remittance flows. At the end of 2008, both spikes reversed and returned to more favorable conditions for remittances.

Besides the Republic of Moldova, all countries experienced a decline or a slowdown in remittance flows during 2008. Furthermore, all countries except the Slovak Republic had increasing remittance flows throughout the years prior to 2008. Once again, these trends are also well explained by GDP trends that are closely linked to monetary policy and the exchange rate. It is difficult, using such a short time series, to extract from these variables additional information about *future* economic trends.

Income

The average nominal wage in the Czech Republic has been steadily increasing, with a slight slowdown in the last two quarters. Setting aside the problem that the average wage might not correctly reflect the wage trends in the sectors in which migrants are employed, it is possible to use the growth rate of the real average wage as an explanatory variable for remittances. Correlations between this index and remittance growth rates vary across countries. Remittances to Ukraine and the Republic of Moldova show no relation to the real wage. Remittances to Vietnam, the Russian Federation, and the Slovak Republic are negatively correlated (–0.34, –0.57, and –0.32, respectively), while those to China and Poland are positively correlated (0.24 and 0.35, respectively). For all countries combined, the correlation is negative, at –0.19. This might go against the theory in the main text, but the problems encountered in this analysis are too vast to take this supposition for granted.

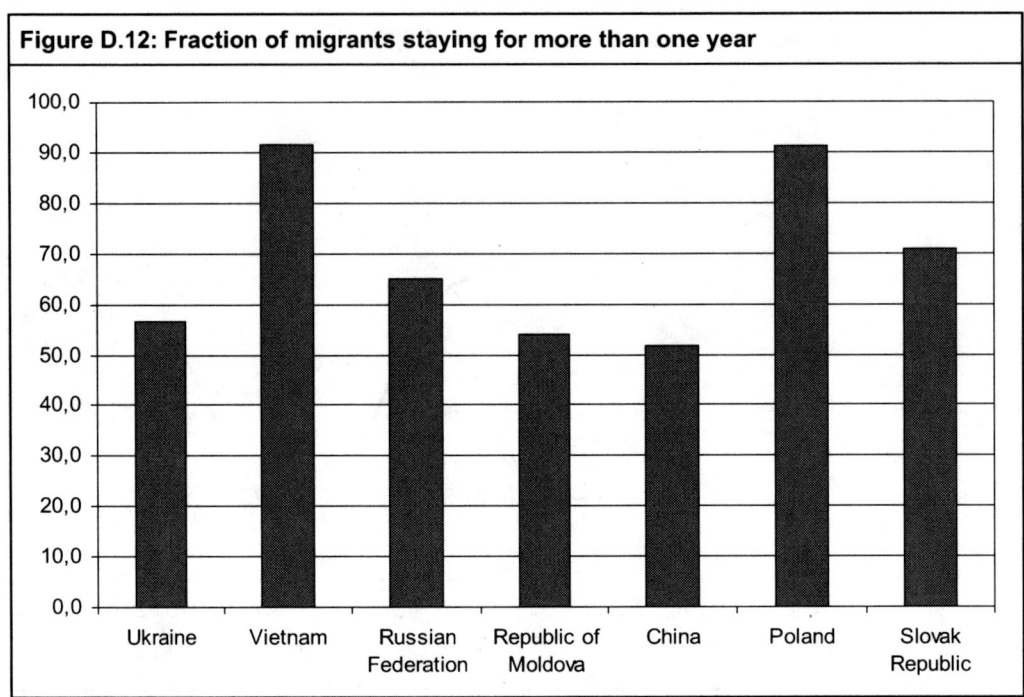

Figure D.12: Fraction of migrants staying for more than one year

Apart from the problem that the average wage might not be a good proxy, as mentioned earlier, the time series sample shrinks by yet another year because the final year's growth rate is not yet known.

Duration of Stay

Figure D.12 shows the proportion of long-term migrants by country.

As theory predicted, there is a slightly negative correlation (–0.2) between the average fraction of long-term migrants and the average level of remittances. However, it should be noted that the level of remittances is steadily growing, and thus taking an average of a growing series might not make much sense. On the other hand, the differences in the levels are quite substantial; hence they are probably not due only to different growth rates.

Sex

There are only three data points for each country (yearly averages of the fraction of women in the migrants), making any analysis of this factor's incidence of this even more difficult.

Country averages (no significant variation in the figures) were compared with the average remittances. As theory predicted, the correlation is negative (–0.26). Once again, the sample of six countries (Ukraine is missing) is extremely small, and results are only roughly indicative of the correlation that might exist between these two averages.

Conclusions

Remittances from the Czech Republic have become a reality since 1993, as the country has moved from being a traditional source of emigrants to a destination for migrants from other countries. Due to a methodological change in data collection in 2005, only time series starting in 2005 are comparable.

Table D.9: Foreigners by sex in the Czech Republic, 2005–2007 (in % of women)

Country	31.12.2005	31.12.2006	31.12.2007
China	43.4	43.4	43.8
Poland	49	47	45.7
Republic of Moldova	37.3	36.6	34.8
Russian Federation	52.7	52.9	52.9
Slovak Republic	40.5	40.2	40.6
Vietnam	38.7	39.2	39.7
Total	41	41.2	41.2
All countries	40.4	40	39.6

Source: Foreigners in the Czech Republic, CSO 2005–2007.

Remittances in the Czech statistics refer to workers' remittances and employees' compensations.

The total amount of annual remittances in the Czech Republic in nominal terms ranges between CZK 36 million to CZK 56 million—i.e., from 1.12 to 1.53 percent of the nominal GDP. The average quarterly remitted amount per capita (all countries combined) is between CZK 28,000 and CZK 34,000.

For all countries except Poland and the Slovak Republic, remittances show an upward trend, with a slowdown in the last two quarters due to the economic crisis. The most important home country for remittances is Ukraine, with a share exceeding 42 percent of the total remitted amount.

Empirical investigation is constrained by a very limited five-year time series, making all analysis highly descriptive. There is little room for understanding simple correlative relationships with other variables and no room for formal econometric analysis. This is especially troublesome, since it is only possible to describe relations between variables separately, with no chance of checking for other effects. Therefore, all conclusions are only partial explanations and only indicative, since it is not possible to differentiate the effects of individual explanatory variables.

Currently, the solution is to group the explanatory variables and make general statements about these categories, rather than obsessively focusing on individual series.

The first set of variables can be summarized as the economic condition of the host country. This set includes GDP, unemployment, and interest and exchange rates. On average at the aggregated level, the relationship between the host country's economic situation and remittances is slightly negative. The level of remittances is inversely proportional to the health of the host economy. However, this aggregate relationship hides a great amount of heterogeneity across countries. It would be interesting to further analyze this heterogeneity and check for other influences, which the current sample does not allow.

The second group of variables could be called demographics and income. In this group are included the number of migrants, the duration of their stay, their sex, and the average (real) wage. These variables seem to account for the level of remittances, which explains the trend of reduced rate of growth or its decline during the last couple of quarters. The strongest variable is the number of migrants. Interestingly, the number of migrants is also pro-cyclical with respect to GDP at business cycle frequencies (again with some heterogeneity across countries).

Variables such as the gender composition and the duration of stay are interesting and could shed light on some small differences between countries, but the sample is far too small to exploit in this regard.

Notes

[1] Based on data from the Czech Ministry of Interior prior to 2005. Since 2005, the CSO bases its methodology for calculating remittances on its own calculation of stocks of migrants. The two approaches are different.

[2] 1. Other countries: established-marked economy (EME), low-income countries (LIC), and developing countries that were not included in the selected individual countries; 2. Total: consolidated group of EME, LIC, and developing countries plus the seven selected countries; 3. All countries: all EME, LIC, developing, and advanced economies combined. After 1989, there was an influx of foreign experts from developed countries, and therefore advanced economies have been included in the aggregated data for comparison purposes.

[3] The CSO does not consider all money transferred abroad by nonresidents as remittances. Nonresidents are individuals residing in the country for less than 12 months.

[4] Countries are in alphabetical order.

[5] "Total" is the sum of all the countries in the previous graphs. "All countries" includes the entire set of data for all countries, whether or not they were included in the previous graphs.

[6] See footnote 1.

[7] Dilip Ratha, Sanket Mohapatra, and Ani Silwai 2009: "Outlook for Remittance flows 2009–2011," *Migration and Development Brief 10*, World Bank.

[8] Seven selected countries by region.

[9] The fraction of migrants is 12.5 and 32 percent respectively, relative to the fraction of remittance flows of 8.3 and 23 percent, respectively.

[10] Since the H-P filter is a two-sided filter, the beginning and end of the filtered series is less representative of the "true" cycle. To avoid the beginning point problem the author used a longer series (starting in 1995).

Annex to Appendix D

Table D.10: Remittances from the Czech Republic, 2005–2009 (CZK millions)

	2005				2006				2007				2008				2009	
	1Q	2Q	3Q	4Q	1Q	2Q	3Q	4Q	1Q	2Q	3Q	4Q	1Q	2Q	3Q	4Q	1Q	2Q
China	26	49	62	73	74	70	71	65	124	133	154	168	127	149	173	231	191	195
Poland	78	106	141	162	269	291	319	375	330	375	451	554	200	262	184	153	332	310
Republic of Moldova	70	147	175	165	193	212	238	241	239	288	337	373	557	647	763	1,037	549	542
Russian Federation	421	455	479	449	398	403	429	449	429	469	506	574	552	562	663	748	708	768
Slovak Republic	3,112	3,679	4,165	4,248	1,833	1,821	1,975	2,109	1,502	1,769	2,025	2,169	1,105	1,033	1,135	1,216	1,729	1,800
Ukraine	2,785	2,901	3,016	2,996	2,725	2,925	3,213	3,400	3,487	3,986	4,559	5,071	4,963	5,151	5,971	5,914	5,596	5,434
Vietnam	519	535	550	564	342	362	380	405	536	589	654	862	1,189	1,199	1,573	1,507	1,433	1,220
Other EMEs and LICs	822	789	793	845	785	879	1,002	1,051	1,099	1,205	1,322	1,860	1,340	1,480	1,762	2,264	1,905	1,801
Total	7,833	8,661	9,381	9,502	6,619	6,963	7,627	8,095	7,746	8,814	10,008	11,631	10,033	10,483	12,224	13,070	12,443	12,070
All countries	9,852	10,666	11,441	11,709	8,024	8,526	9,311	9,920	9,288	10,516	11,890	13,309	12,622	13,138	14,347	15,470	14,697	14,382

Table D.11: Stock of migrants in the Czech Republic, 2005–2006

	2005				2006				2007				2008				2009	
	1Q	2Q	3Q	4Q	1Q	2Q	3Q	4Q	1Q	2Q	3Q	4Q	1Q	2Q	3Q	4Q	1Q	2Q
China	1,004	1,557	1,712	1,906	2,434	2,425	2,360	2,273	4,127	4,238	4,394	4,711	3,895	4,480	4,563	5,356	5,095	5,111
Poland	13,641	13,936	15,038	16,333	16,293	16,717	17,540	19,015	21,700	23,440	25,084	27,460	21,037	21,370	22,739	22,002	22,639	22,415
Republic of Moldova	3,165	4,466	4,893	4,832	6,832	7,189	7,480	7,847	6,542	7,045	7,616	7,944	15,180	17,406	17,530	21,434	11,070	11,025
Russian Federation	15,529	15,892	16,507	16,869	17,221	17,883	18,446	19,057	19,794	20,753	21,870	23,232	24,075	24,111	25,124	27,795	28,042	29,070
Slovak Republic	81,708	89,880	100,040	102,379	106,416	110,747	116,212	120,873	120,608	125,338	129,553	132,867	133,332	135,567	157,368	136,545	129,715	130,002
Ukraine	79,669	82,397	85,314	88,046	89,957	93,661	97,366	101,078	106,964	112,549	120,313	126,324	126,261	127,384	135,071	132,262	133,759	134,550
Vietnam	34,934	35,562	36,280	36,907	37,431	38,450	39,466	40,488	42,625	44,671	46,381	50,028	52,883	53,421	59,243	60,404	61,075	61,278
Other EMEs and LICs	32,960	32,131	31,433	31,857	36,988	38,165	39,536	40,590	42,644	44,407	47,516	64,265	53,474	57,179	57,345	62,665	60,757	60,560
Total	262,610	275,821	291,217	299,129	313,572	325,187	338,406	351,221	365,024	382,441	402,727	436,831	430,137	440,928	479,673	468,463	452,152	454,011
All countries	295,814	309,964	326,363	335,307	347,792	360,830	375,510	389,793	406,906	426,373	449,213	476,097	484,085	481,644	498,217	508,378	507,483	508,576

Table D.12: Duration of stay of migrants in the Czech Republic, 2005–2006 (in % number of migrants staying longer than 1 year)

	2005				2006				2007				2008				2009	
	1Q	2Q	3Q	4Q	1Q	2Q	3Q	4Q	1Q	2Q	3Q	4Q	1Q	2Q	3Q	4Q	1Q	2Q
China	55.9	37.1	35.7	33.7	48.4	53.1	56.3	57.7	62.2	61.2	57.1	53.6	56.9	60.4	51.5	46.9	52.3	53.1
Poland	94.6	92.2	89.4	88.7	92.1	91.5	91.4	90.1	91.4	91.9	89.5	88.6	88.9	85.9	91.1	93	94.7	97.2
Republic of Moldova	72.9	55.3	52.4	53.5	63.5	62.9	60.5	64	55.1	49.7	45.8	43.4	56.5	58.7	49.9	44.7	38.8	42.4
Russian Federation	57.7	56.4	56.5	62.8	64.5	66.6	66.8	67	68.3	68.4	68.9	68.1	69.1	68.6	64.7	65.5	67	66.8
Slovak Republic	46.5	45.6	42.6	43.5	74.2	75.4	76.5	76.1	81.9	80.8	80.2	81.2	79.2	80.5	70.1	79.8	81.1	81.2
Ukraine	53.7	55	57	60.9	62.5	62.4	61.5	61	61.7	58.5	56.2	54.3	53.7	53.5	51	50.6	52	56.8
Vietnam	96.2	96.8	97.1	97.7	97.8	97.8	97.8	97.4	96.7	95.8	94.3	89.2	82.3	81.9	75.9	79.2	83.3	91.1
Other EMEs and LICs	58.1	64.3	68.7	67.7	70.4	67.4	63.9	63.2	45.9	44.8	45.6	51.4	36.2	36.8	27.2	26	42.1	36.7
Total	60.8	60.3	59.7	61.5	73.4	74.8	73.3	73	74.1	72.7	71.3	69.9	69.2	69.6	66.1	65.8		
All countries	60.3	60.1	59.8	61.4	72.4	73	72.7	72.7	73.9	72.6	71.5	69.6	68.9	68	67.3	75.4	69.1	71.7

Eco-Audit

Environmental Benefits Statement

The World Bank is committed to preserving Endangered Forests and natural resources. We print World Bank Working Papers and Country Studies on postconsumer recycled paper, processed chlorine free. The World Bank has formally agreed to follow the recommended standards for paper usage set by Green Press Initiative—a nonprofit program supporting publishers in using fiber that is not sourced from Endangered Forests. For more information, visit www.greenpressinitiative.org.

In 2008, the printing of these books on recycled paper saved the following:

Trees*	Solid Waste	Water	Net Greenhouse Gases	Total Energy
289	8,011	131,944	27,396	92 mil.
*40 feet in height and 6–8 inches in diameter	Pounds	Gallons	Pounds CO_2 Equivalent	BTUs